WHAT PEOPLE ARE SAYING ABOUT
The Essential Guide for Families with Down Syndrome

Plans and Actions for Independence at Every Stage of Life

"As with most families with children who have a disability, this book is created out of the love and experience of a father who knows there are many parents who need this information at any age through their journey. Great read and great resources."
Barbara Bush, President, Solutions for Special Needs Families

"In *The Essential Guide*, Steve validates our emotions as parents, acknowledges our fears, and gives us practical tips to accommodate the need all individuals have to be autonomous, self-reliant and self-worthy. I recommend this book for all caregivers to those with special needs regardless of age. As parents, we are the experts of our loved ones, and this is an excellent resource in navigating our own decisions to better support the goals and dreams of those we love."
Tara Goodwin, D.O., Adult Down syndrome Clinic Questcare Dallas

"I believe your resource book will be a pinnacle resource 'go-to' for generations. It's a MUST HAVE for everyone who's been chosen to be in our situation, because our children don't come with manuals, or even milestone suggestions. It makes me sad to think about how many parents and caregiver feel, or will feel, the overwhelming sense I did in NOT knowing what to do next on this journey. That's the reason this project of yours is so important! It gives direction

to parents who need guidance along the way. While people are seeking the right way to go, this book will be a beacon on a dark path!"
Stacy Lynn, parent of 16-year-old Slayton

"[*The Essential Guide*] will be an invaluable aid to families to help plan for the future from when their child is young."
Ruth Hewitt, retired speech therapist

"The goal of every parent is to prepare their children for the demands of life. *The Essential Guide for Families with Down Syndrome* provides critical guidance and tips to help ensure every individual with Down syndrome leads the most independent and successful life as possible. Steve Friedman addresses important issues that impact individuals with Down syndrome across the lifespan ranging from education and social relationships to financial well-being. I am confident this book will serve as a valuable reference and guide to families for years to come."
Dr. Joe Ryan, Ph.D., Sue Stanzione Distinguished Professorship for ClemsonLIFE

"As a longstanding organization serving adults with I/DD, there's rarely a time that we don't hear about the tenacity that families must have to find resources for their loved ones around the country. Steve and his incredible family have put together a resource to help families thrive, and help parents find their identity in raising an amazing individual who has access to the care and programs they need."
Becca McPherson, VP of Development, Marbridge Foundation

"This practical guidebook lays out the critical steps for building independence. Steve Friedman provides comprehensive planning tools, paired with thoughtful parent perspectives. This is a great resource which covers all areas of life for individuals with Down syndrome along with their families."

Teresa Unnerstall, DS-ASD Consultant and author of *A New Course: A Mother's Journey Navigating Down Syndrome and Autism*

"I'm so thankful for this resource that Steve has put together. It's like no other. Once you start reading it's not easy to put it down. My reference book now (although it's much more than that) and the one I'll be recommending to other families."

Rosaura, parent of 17-year-old Ethan S.

The Essential Guide for Families with Down Syndrome

Plans and Actions for Independence at Every Stage of Life

Sally,
It's never too early to
nor too late to
plan for independence.

All the best,
Steve

Steve Friedman

The Essential Guide for Families with Down Syndrome

Plans and Actions for Independence at Every Stage of Life

Steve Friedman

Peavine Press, LLC
Austin, Texas

Publisher: Peavine Press, LLC

Austin, Texas USA

www.BeyondDownSyndrome.net

BeyondDownSyndrome@gmail.com

ISBN: 978-1-7342211-8-3 (ebook), 978-1-7342211-9-0 (paper),

Library of Congress Catalog Number: 2022922731

Cover image credit: Jennuine Expressions, LLC

FREE BONUS – Complimentary checklists and worksheets available at http://www.beyonddownsyndrome.net/The-Essential-Guide

Contents

DEDICATION

Gwendolyn is my hero. Except for the fact that she's my daughter, you might think this odd. She's half my age, has disabilities, is oftentimes labeled stubborn, and appears to lack the initiative and optimism I pride myself on.

But Gwendolyn *is* my hero. Contrary to superficial impressions, she is very energetic, creative, and a go-getter. She can dance for hours and sing for even longer. She has the initiative to sort coupons for unnamed GIs halfway around the world and the ambition to be Cinderella. She chases her own independence and craves the joy of friendship and love!

And what I admire the very most about Gwendolyn is that she is untainted by societal norms. When she was young, if she didn't want to walk, she would merely stop and sit. She doesn't care about fashion standards as she wears mixed socks, her Hannah Montana wig, and her own unique mix of shirts and pants. She says what she thinks. She loves people who make her feel good and disregards those that don't provide positive energy to her. When she is REALLY in her "zone," she shows it with unabashed glee. When at a concert or talking about her boyfriend(s) and their plans, she shows such happiness that I don't think anyone can smile wider with their whole face joining in!

Sometimes I wonder what my life would be like if I emulated such rare traits, even occasionally.

Gwendolyn truly does it her way. She may know no other way, but she is who she is, takes immense pride in that, and wouldn't change a thing in enjoying her life's ride. And I wouldn't change a thing either.

Thanks Gwendolyn. I dedicate this book, and the path that it paves for others, to you.

Love, Dad

Introduction

"She Has Down Syndrome!"

We had only arrived at the hospital an hour before. Things were happening fast. There was no time for an epidural. The doctor had not arrived. Jennifer insisted she needed to start pushing. The nurse relented, indicating at least a half hour of labor lay ahead. I held Jennifer's hand as she bore into her first push. Suddenly, a head popped out. Astonished, I remarked, "There sure is a lot of hair on that head!"

The nurse screamed, "STOP!" as she rushed over from the corner of the room. Gwendolyn wasted no time in coming into this world. My eyes glazed over as I snipped the umbilical cord that began Gwendolyn's independence journey. However, when she lay on Jennifer's lap and their eyes connected, Jennifer exclaimed, "She has Down syndrome!"

When Gwendolyn was born in 1994, we went through the normal circuit of shock, fear, sadness, guilt, concern, and love. We assumed all our dreams and plans would have to be replaced. We delved into stacks of books on raising newborns with Down syndrome while we contacted local Down syndrome organizations and public health resources. Soon, we were overwhelmed with advice. We decided to step back and just love our new baby.

Every family follows their own journey, navigating their own challenges while learning about their loved one's specific needs. This doesn't happen overnight. It is a lifelong adventure.

Independence became our top priority when Gwendolyn's public school experience was coming to an end at age 18. While school was far from perfect, she learned a lot, just as we did. We had grown accustomed to the counselors framing the next year, the teachers guiding her through her learning maze, and the school occupying most of Gwendolyn's waking hours. But as high school drew to a close, it felt like we were about to fall off a cliff. We felt lost. We felt behind. There were no guardrails for what was next. We needed to quickly figure out the next stage of her life.

A Timely Angel

As the end of Gwendolyn's high school years jolted us into frenetic future planning, we recognized two major lessons:

1. This should have been a lifelong plan, established years before and adjusted along the way. Our piecemeal, short-term planning was not preparing Gwendolyn or the family for the many changes ahead.
2. This plan could not be *my* plan. It was a family plan but most importantly, it was Gwendolyn's Independence Plan.

The family gathered to put a path together. It started with a simple question that had been absent for eighteen years: "Gwendolyn, what do you want?"

Gwendolyn has always been a strong-willed dreamer, but her response surprised us. "I want to be independent!"

Our immediate post-high school dilemma was resolved by an angel. We were fortunate to reunite with a local Down syndrome advocate, Rosa Rocha, who had just started the Friends of Down Syndrome (FoDS), a Houston organization that now serves over fifty adults with Down syndrome. The organization's day program provides a learning and social environment that supports the ambitions and abilities of adults with Down syndrome. Rosa's passion quickly made us believers. Gwendolyn shifted to FoDS upon graduation from high school. This was a positive step on her journey that sprang up just when we needed it. But was this it? Would this satisfy the long-term ambitions of independence brewing inside Gwendolyn?

Call for Independence

The average life span of people with Down syndrome has stretched from merely twelve years in the 1940s[1] to twenty-five years in 1983 and now currently sixty years[2], largely due to "access to improved medical technologies" from birth through adulthood[3] and greater focus on lifelong development. This is truly uplifting news for the Down syndrome community. **More learning, social relationships, work experiences, and inclusive opportunities abound. But new health, financial, and housing challenges arise as adults with Down syndrome now often outlive their parents.** This should act as a catalyst for discussions about independence for our loved ones. The call for independence has never been stronger.

Defining Independence

Independence is a freeing aspiration for everyone. The word suggests individualism, self-reliance, and self-determination. It also implies pride, comfort, and joy. Yet creating that independence is far from easy. Even for our neurotypical children, building these skills and then letting go is not simple, no matter how prepared they are or how willing we are.

It is no different for our loved ones with Down syndrome. **Independence means something different for every person and family.** Independence is personal hygiene and helping around the house. Independence may mean going to work, attending continuing education, or working out at the gym by themselves. Independence may also include taking advantage of the growing variety of community home options, too. These varying levels of autonomy depend less upon age and more upon abilities, as well as the comfort and confidence of the individual and their parents or caregivers. More than ever before, people with Down syndrome aspire to have that same independence their siblings and friends enjoy. They are also advocating for themselves—voicing their dreams and wishes to others.

Your Independence Team

Down syndrome is not just an additional twenty-first chromosome of one person, it is a condition that affects the whole family. As such, we are all thrust into tackling the various lifelong challenges and celebrating the glorious achievements together. We can't do this alone. We need a support team to bring different expertise, experiences, and ideas to the table. We need people who understand the challenges and aspirations, who will lend a caring ear but will also kick us in the rear when the going gets tough and we need to push boundaries. We need an Independence Team.

The team consists of you, the family with Down syndrome, and various support members. **The captain of your Independence Team is your person with Down syndrome. We will call this person, regardless of age, the *self-advocate* or *loved one*.** They

4

must drive the process with their interests and passions, aspirations, and dreams.

The rest of the family—parents, siblings, grandparents, aunts, and uncles—as well as teachers, doctors, and therapists are advisors. You may not be a professional doctor, social worker, or educator, but you are an expert on your son or daughter. Hence, it is up to the parents or primary caregivers to educate everyone else, to dispel long-held beliefs and stereotypes about people with Down syndrome, and to encourage everyone to think big! It is also your responsibility to invite new valuable advisors into the team and to dismiss those who don't believe. The Independence Team guides the process, and it starts with our loved one at the center of it all.

This guidebook is here to provide the path and direction for your team's success.

The UPLifting Guidebook Project

Throughout Gwendolyn's independence journey, it became obvious that the path was not clear, for us or others. The resources to present opportunities and challenges, help evaluate options, and guide us on where and when to get started were absent. I created a website to document our family's journey and initiated a family survey to understand the hopes and dreams, as well as the perceived obstacles and challenges, of people with Down syndrome and their caregivers. The UPLifting Guidebook Project was born.

Nearly every family dreams of independence and self-sufficiency. However, the Survey[4] revealed that 60 percent are overwhelmed by the prospect and aren't sure where to turn or even how to get started while 35 percent are unsure of the financial resources required and how to secure them. My family's frustrations were apparently shared by many.

In an effort to simplify and outline the process of exploring independence, I consulted with experts and organizations, as well as hundreds of families. The Project promotes lifelong opportunities and inspires mindset shifts toward one of independence and possibilities.

Independence means something different for each person and family. I don't suggest that my family's journey should be your path. My goal is to share the many avenues for independence, including personal building blocks, education, work, and home living in order to provide you with the information you need to make the best decisions for your family.

The UPLifting Guidebook Project sprouted from Gwendolyn's amazing journey, but it is more than just Gwendolyn's story. It is your story.

It Takes a Village

In the pages ahead I share my family's accomplishments and triumphs. I also humbly confess our mistakes and omissions. We can all agree that parenting a firstborn, not to mention a child with disabilities, is an immense challenge. We did our best but in retrospect, there are certain decisions, approaches, and habits we would have changed throughout the years. This isn't easy for any of us. This book shares both the successes and learnings along the way but it also serves as a reminder that none of us are perfect. We all do our best given the curveballs life throws at us.

It has been my great fortune to meet so many amazing families throughout this Project. In the pages ahead and through **Family Features** at the end of each chapter, you will hear from thirteen different families about their experiences and aspirations. Each one would agree they are striving for independence in their own way.

Dutch lives in an apartment with a support roommate. Fionn is an entrepreneur and spokesman working with his dad. Amanda and Slayton share the chores and hobbies they do to build their independence. Daniel and Camille cultivate strong social skills and enjoy meeting others. Meanwhile, Ayla, Chaya, and Ethan are managing the challenges of dual diagnosis Down syndrome and autism or post-pandemic regression, yet they continue to build their independent skills and vision. Noah benefits from the detailed planning and aggressive learning approach of his mom, just as Dale enjoys the confidence his mother instills upon him by encouraging his independence through unconventional means.

Some are toddlers and teens while others are in their twenties or thirties. Some work and many are in school or day programs. Some are developing a strong, independent environment at home while others have established their home within the community. You may recognize yourself in these stories and will certainly be inspired to carry the torch of independence with your own self-advocate.

Additionally, many experts share their knowledge throughout the book with focused **Expert Advice** on critical topics such as health, financial resources, education, and safety to ensure you are prepared for the road ahead. Further information is provided in an extensive **Resources** section at the back of the book to supplement your reading and provide you with contacts for implementing your plan.

Your Independence Plan

This guidebook provides concrete direction for your entire Independence Team. Self-advocates, parents, and caregivers can lean on this Guide to develop the skills, analyze options, and make prudent choices in support of independence. Other team members will perhaps gain the insights to teach and practice differently, to best support the journey of those with Down syndrome and other intellectual/developmental disabilities (I/DD). By the end of the book, you will have a clear and achievable plan to realize the desired level of independence for your loved one with Down syndrome and your supporting family as well.

Your Independence Plan is the compilation of your goals and the steps along the way toward family success. An Independence Plan template is provided as a free download along with other complimentary worksheets at www.beyonddownsyndrome. net/The-Essential-Guide for you to use as documentation and consideration for your journey ahead.

How to Use This Guidebook

No matter where you are in your journey of independence, you'll find essential advice and resources that will save you time, money, and angst. Reading this Guide will provide you with keen awareness of and planning for the adventure ahead. At the beginning of each section, specific actions will be highlighted based on your loved one's stage of life. The resources and index at the back of the book enable easy reference when searching for specific information throughout your excursion.

The Essential Guide is not about tackling the milestones of newborns with Down syndrome or guiding parents through school administrative meetings. You can find plenty of quality books available for those critical steps. This book is about fostering *independence* for your loved one with Down syndrome, so they are best prepared to achieve their dreams with confidence and pride.

The guidebook includes five sections:

1. **Mindset Shifts:** We may be overwhelmed by the profundity of the situation when our child is born. But shifting our mindset from life changes, limitations, and broken dreams to one of opportunities and achievements should happen before your self-advocate turns twenty or independence is thrust upon them due to other family changes. In this section, you will find advice on shifting your mindset to foster independence throughout the household from the earliest of ages.

2. **Fostering Independence:** Section II covers a wide range of mechanisms to develop an independence skill set through activities, choices, and decision-making, in order to build the confidence of your self-advocate and the whole family.

3. **Foundations for the Future:** Experts contribute essential information about common health challenges for adults with Down syndrome and how to best prepare for them. An Independence Plan is not free. In this section, you will find a comprehensive guide to the financial resources available, how and when to apply for each, and how to avoid traps that may jeopardize your benefits. These chapters provide you with the foundation to consider education, work, and living options for the future.

4. **Taking on the World:** Most self-advocates and their families seek community inclusion opportunities. This section explores education, work, and community integration prospects and the resources available to achieve them.

5. **Home Is Where the Heart Is:** This final section empowers you and your self-advocate to consider all residential

options, from the family home to community living and a home of their own. You will find the pros and cons of various options, and the steps to make your choice a reality.

Start Now!

It would have been great for my family to have developed this plan years ago. Nevertheless, when the time came, it required a shift in our thinking. It required us to put more faith in Gwendolyn and be prepared to let go. We knew it would take time to tackle the plan to the satisfaction of Gwendolyn and ourselves, but this would be the greatest gift we could ever give Gwendolyn. So, we started.

Over the past few years, Gwendolyn has learned a lot. Her face beamed with pride when she ran her first load of wash. She now makes eggs and bacon for breakfast "by myself." She loves to work and "bring home the bacon." She walked to work and biked around the nearby park all by herself. Now she lives in a fabulous living community that supports her growth and independence. When I ask Gwendolyn who is the most important person in her Independence Plan, she proclaims, "I am!" And when I ask if she is proud of herself, with a glimmer in her eye she says, "Yes, I am. I love myself!"

It is never too early, nor too late to begin contemplating, planning, and making choices to foster the independence that breeds confidence and success for adults with Down syndrome. Let's start this journey together.

SECTION I
MINDSET SHIFTS

There are 7.37 million people in the US with intellectual/developmental disabilities (I/DD), a number slightly greater than the population of the state of Arizona.[5] This guidebook samples a wide variety of stories and perspectives. While everyone's story is unique, two themes stand out through discussions with our **Family Features**: the parent's optimistic perspective and the focus and inclusion of their loved one with Down syndrome. These appear to be best practices, so we will begin our journey there.

An optimistic perspective is natural for some caregivers and difficult for others. Certainly, the abrupt change in family plans does give reason to pause. Yet, as much as the negativity of one person can bring a room down, **a positive outlook can elevate the possible to reality**. It helps everyone on the Independence Team to believe and to chase the many opportunities that are afforded our kids in this modern age. Chapter 1 will explore the parent's perspective and their roles in making the future brighter.

Additionally, placing your loved one with Down syndrome at the center of discussions and decisions on matters that concern them is essential. Chapter 2 will introduce the person-centered planning model, how to foster this approach within your family, and with schools, doctors, and the broader community.

Our children with Down syndrome have a long life of growth and development ahead. Though their slope or rate of accelerated learning is often gentler, their cap or ceiling remains high. As adults, our loved ones are no longer transitioning from crawling to walking, but their transformation from dependency to independence accelerates. They are both evolving their skills and managing the conflict between comfort and change. These may not be easy times and can introduce developmental stalls or plateaus. We will discuss how to recognize these plateaus and how to help nudge our self-advocates onward.

Whatever your dreams and aspirations, independence is defined by your self-advocate with encouragement from their Independence Team.

Section I: Plans and Actions		
#	Action	Life Stage*
1	Download your Independence Plan template	Early Childhood
2	Form and convene the Independence Team	Early Childhood
3	Ensure a positive, person-centered perspective	Early Childhood
4	Create an independence mind map	Adolescence
5	Know the signs of plateauing	Childhood

If your loved one has passed this stage but has not completed this action, place this at the top of your action plan

Check out resources and references at the back of the book. Downloads are available for free at:

http://www.beyonddownsyndrome.net/The-Essential-Guide

Chapter 1
Parent's Perspective

The world has changed and the possibilities are endless. Now, our children with Down syndrome have countless services available, from speech and occupational therapy in their first days of life to focused life skills classes and inclusion throughout their school years. Adults with Down syndrome are getting jobs, going to college, getting married, and living on their own. The opportunities and support systems are expanding rapidly, and the aura of confidence on their beaming faces is proof society is on the right path.

These positive changes summon the need for greater planning in preparation for the opportunities ahead, as well as for the medical and financial burdens relegated to those that live longer. As a vital member of the Independence Team, it is incumbent upon you to navigate the obstacles and unknowns to unlock these grand opportunities for your loved ones. The days of the R-word and shipping people off to institutions, more to protect a fragile society than to provide for the disabled, are largely behind us.

As Amanda's mom Joyce asserts, "Everything we strive to teach our children is working toward their independence from the moment they are born."

We are the generations that must shift mindset toward the possibilities and chase them with vigor and determination.

Not "OR" but "AND"

We can all acknowledge that the idea of independence for our children with Down syndrome is exciting but not easy. They are equipped with different skills; they are a bit naïve to societal norms and especially the evil that can lurk. They can be easy prey for those without scruples. Yet, we must find the right balance.

Ms. Smith is a senior teacher of math and social skills at the Friends of Down Syndrome in Houston, which employs a multifaceted "WAVES" (Wellness, Academics, Vocational, Education, Social Engagement) program for its fifty adults with Down syndrome. Ms. Smith implores, "I wish parents could take a class because some of them hinder their kids…because [they] shelter them and protect them so much." Some people have a theory that we are putting our child at risk by advocating for independence; how can they be safe *and* independent?

The answer to that question starts with the parent or caregiver. We must believe in independence before our child with Down syndrome can even crawl. Then we need to instill our loved ones with skills and experiences to prepare them to be independent and advocate for themselves. Finally, we need to carefully select day programs, social circles, work opportunities, and living arrangements to ensure a proper level of safety and security is provided based on our loved one's ability to discern risks and make prudent decisions themselves. Regardless of the level of independence your loved one ultimately achieves, there is a plethora of opportunities for the wide range of abilities within the Down syndrome community.

Thus, we are establishing their independence with personalized handrails. We can help discover and create a safe environment that supports their growth and flourishing. And now is perhaps the best time of all to pursue this path.

Lean Toward "Similar"

Another frame of mind to consider is our natural compulsion to compare, specifically expectations and abilities. It is natural from the very first day for us to identify the differences that our new son or daughter with Down syndrome may have—the physical differences and the slow rate of progress. At times, we may lament the differences between our child and their siblings or our friends' kids. We may focus on how our child's future and indeed our own future will now be different. These thoughts are natural, but not beneficial. Consider them briefly and then put them in a box and begin to reframe your mindset.

Honestly, your path will not be the same as others. Some may dispute that statement and I'm certainly encouraging you to strive for your dreams and those of your self-advocate, but I also want us to be grounded in a reality that supports those dreams, not disillusions. You will have new challenges—health challenges, school disagreements, longer lead times to accomplish tasks, and most certainly extra financial burdens as well.

Rather than focus on "different" or even the idealistic "same," lean into "similar." Their high school experience may not be the same as their peers, but it doesn't have to be so different. Nor does a college experience or vocational opportunity. While their independence will not be the same as others, it can be equally rewarding. Your child with Down syndrome can achieve many wonderful things in their life. It starts with a positive mindset, in believing, in striving to make those possibilities reality. And as you achieve these goals, your child with Down syndrome will become their own self-advocate, and you will become a more confident parent and sponsor.

"It's Never Too Early"

At first glance, this guidebook might appear to be targeted to families of adults with Down syndrome. That was my expectation before I began this project, largely because that was our family experience. We were not well prepared for life after high school. Surprisingly, Gwendolyn knew exactly what she wanted—independence! And she'd been telling us all along—first by no longer needing us to stay with her at social events and later by cutting out pictures of furniture she wanted for her future home. We just had to listen.

But it was admittedly a shock to the system. My wife, Jennifer, and I consider ourselves rather progressive parents—open-minded, supportive, encouraging of our kids to try new things, make mistakes, and learn without the protective parental umbrella. But this didn't always extend to Gwendolyn and certainly didn't extend to our thinking of her working and moving out of the house one day. To suddenly consider these leaps at eighteen was a difficult paradigm shift. We soon realized it would have been easier to foster that independence from the outset; to have employment and independent living as goals before Gwendolyn was even a toddler and to use those goals to develop specific skills to support those aspirations. Preparing Gwendolyn with more independent tasks and choices both at home and at school through future-focused an Individualized Education Program (IEP) could have made Gwendolyn's transition toward greater independence in her teens and twenties more seamless. Additionally, the rest of our family would have been better prepared to envision a future of successful independence.

Have independent expectations from the start. Consider every aspect of your loved one's years ahead through an independence lens and ensure his or her growth and development supports that approach.

"It's Never Too Late"

Instead, we as parents had to catch up. We had to assess Gwendolyn's skills gaps and our knowledge gaps as well, and then focus on closing those spaces so we would all be prepared for her burgeoning independence path. And I know we are not alone.

Families with Down syndrome are in a wide variety of places. Some have been preparing for independence for years and others have turned a blind eye to the prospect. Perhaps when your child was born the opportunities for kids and adults with disabilities were more restrictive. Maybe your location offers fewer occupation/physical/speech therapy services, not to mention positive community support, so a vision of limited opportunities naturally evolved.

But even if your child is twenty-five, thirty-five, or forty-five, it is not too late to consider a path of independence. The prospects in the modern world are tremendous. Our loved ones are seeking these opportunities even more. And with the life span for people with Down syndrome double what it was in the 1980s[6] many of our loved ones will now outlive their parents. Independence is more essential now than ever.

Perhaps the sense of urgency is greater, and the transition more difficult as an adult, but the reward for our self-advocates will still be worth it. Even if your loved one is at an advanced age, I suggest diving in to Section II on building independence. Foster that independence at home, shift your mindset, and share the possibilities with your self-advocate. Choosing a new path can be scary but will support your loved one's progress and your own future planning as well.

Our UPL Family Survey found the two most significant barriers to independence were a lack of available guidance and parental mindset. Too many of us can't envision life with an independent, largely self-sufficient self-advocate that may not live at home. When your mindset shifts and you are equipped with the step-by-step plan in this guidebook, the possibilities become endless.

Parental Roles

Ours is not a role dominated by coddling and protection. That may be a primary focus during the initial days or weeks, but it gradually declines, replaced by more empowering roles such as teacher, supporter, and dream champion.

Teacher

Our children are equipped only with instinctual motions and underlying DNA in those early years. We are their teachers. We choose what to show them, what to tell them, what love is, and what danger may be. We also decide what not to show or tell them. We are their filter on the world. From this, they learn what *we* choose with little of their own take on life in these early years. Most psychologists and educators agree that these preadolescent years are the most formative for any child.[7] We have the opportunity to not only teach them right from wrong, but also about choices and possibilities as opposed to merely following rules and societal norms that can restrict options or ambitions. As the most important advisor on the Independence Team, we are the lead teachers of skills, abilities, and mindset.

Supporter

Our supporting role is important because we provide the safety net in case of danger or mistakes. The word "supporter" also implies we are not the "doer." Generally, **the more we teach and support but let them do the task, the more they learn and the greater confidence they will have in their own abilities.** These are the seeds of strength and independence that all our kids need.

No one, even the most experiences doctors and teachers, knows your loved one like you do. Hence, we are called upon to roll up our sleeves and advocate for our loved ones to ensure they have the best environment to learn and grow—on the playground, in school, in the doctor's office, and when searching for jobs or living arrangements.

As the key advisors on the Independence Team, we are charged with ensuring ideas are developed, evaluated, improved, and implemented. Creativity and challenge within the Independence Team will help strengthen the plan, but negativity and skepticism will only drag your team down.

Dream Champion

Dreaming. What a lovely word. Dreaming has gotten lost in our fast-paced, results-oriented world. Yet we all benefit from dreaming. Contemplating our futures. Recognizing our strengths and passions. Driving ourselves to achieve what will make us happiest.

Today, not only do we require time to dream, we need to also have the positive mindset to park the stereotypes, harsh realities, or naysayers to the side. Those that say our children can't learn, love, and live independently either need to be convinced otherwise, or removed from the circle of trust. We need those who, at their core, *believe* in the prospects. Optimistic approaches will unlock all the possibilities in the minds of our self-advocates, but also ourselves, our families, and other supportive members of your Independence Team. We are our child's cheerleaders, encouraging them to believe in themselves, to explore, and to follow their interests. Fostering this mindset early on will breed confidence and determination. Otherwise, it is very hard to create this approach during adulthood when it may require a 180-degree turn from a more limited attitude and outlook. That's the recipe for undiscovered dreams and unfulfilled opportunities.

Moving Forward

Today there are countless opportunities for kids and adults with Down syndrome. We may have to do a lot of research and push against norms and boundaries, but the future of our self-advocates is in their hands…and in your hands. Your mindset will determine how much of the opportunities and dreams are embraced and eventually realized. As parents, your role is to be the catalyst rather than the restraint. Your reward is immeasurable in the strength, pride, and independence of your self-advocates.

Certainly, the path is not always easy or well-defined. Those self-advocates and families with ambition, determination, and resourcefulness are rewarded with opportunities and success. Those that get stuck in the paradigms of the past or the quagmire of options now available miss out on many of the new prospects. The remaining sections of this guidebook will help you understand the options and pave the path forward. However, the ambition and determination must come from you and your self-advocate.

In our first **Family Feature**, Stephanie shares their story of determination, early planning, and life lessons that have supported the growth of their son, Noah (age four).

Family Feature
Noah's Story

Noah was born in June 2018, and we had no idea that he was going to have Down syndrome. He spent fifteen days in the NICU and on day ten we were told he had Down syndrome based on his chromosomal karyotype. The genetics counselor gave us a sad look and said "I am so sorry, but your son has trisomy 21 and will need therapy. He will probably not walk until he is four and most likely be nonverbal." This statement caused his dad and me a lot of grief and anger. You see, Noah's dad and I are both very stubborn and took her words as a challenge. We never back down from a challenge. We did not want pity or any other negative emotion that people gave us based on his diagnosis because he was more than his diagnosis. While his dad processed this information at a rapid pace, it took me a little longer and I grieved for the "perfect" baby I thought I was having. Little did I know that he was the "perfect" baby, perfect for us!

Starting Early

I got to work researching Down syndrome. I contacted a friend that had an older child with Down syndrome, and I asked her what

I needed to do to make my son as independent as possible. Her first piece of advice was to love him and then to get into contact with an early intervention program as soon as possible.

Noah was released from NICU on July 5, 2018. The following Monday I was on the phone with Birth to Three scheduling an appointment for evaluation. We began occupational and developmental therapy when Noah was twenty-six days. From then on, my days were spent scouring the internet and making connections via Facebook. His dad and I made a pact to do anything and everything possible to ensure that our child had every advantage he could get to lead a productive and INDEPENDENT life!

Noah is now four and he has been walking since he was roughly sixteen months old. He started saying words around age two. We are constantly looking for therapy-based toys that will strengthen his grasp and fine motor skills. We go to a Down syndrome clinic yearly, meeting with a behavioral pediatrician and a myriad of therapists to ensure that we are doing all that we need to do so that Noah has every opportunity to be independent and self-sufficient.

Planning for the Future

I am a planner so I thought about as many possibilities as I could. I asked myself the following questions:

1. **Who** will provide care for Noah and not abuse or take advantage of him?
2. **Where** will he live if his dad and I are gone?
3. **How** will he get to his appointments, grocery store, or work?
4. **What** do we need to do to prepare for all the above?

For the first, we intend to secure guardianship at age eighteen with several alternatives to keep him out of state care. I need to make sure that my child will be taken care of if something happens to us. He has siblings but I don't think his siblings should have to take care of him. I have in place someone to be his guardian if his dad and I are no longer present to care for him. We have life insurance policies that will provide a means of caring for him in the event of our demise. I have discussed all of this with my oldest son (twenty-one) and he is in agreement with the way my life insurance will be divided between him and his brother.

As far as the other three questions, that will be based on his level of independence. He will inherit the house we own if that is feasible or else look at assisted living communities that meet his needs and our expectations. The "how" will come over time as he develops, making choices and decisions more obvious. The end goal is independence with as little interference as possible.

Life Lessons

The advice that I have received that has held true is that our kids do all the things that neurotypical kids do but in their own time. While this is hard to take sometimes, it is true. Things that we see as their struggle, they don't see it as a struggle because that is just the way it is for them. It is <u>their</u> normal. Everything that our other kids have done, Noah is doing or starting to do. To raise a truly independent child with Down syndrome is to give them every opportunity that other children get. Teach them to read, teach them to write, to walk, run, dress and undress, bathe, and groom themselves. It will not be easy, but it will be worthwhile!

Find yourselves the one person that connects with your child and watch how your child blooms! Socialization through day care and school has been a major help in aiding Noah in reaching milestones because he sees other children doing things and then he wants to do what they are doing. He watches them intently then attempts to copy them until he gets it right. Encourage this behavior and reward it!

Above all, expect your child to be successful. Do not set limits on them because if you do then success will not be achieved. Our kids can do absolutely anything they want if they are given the appropriate tools and support for success.

We do not take "no" for an answer. If we are told "no," we seek out a second or third opinion. Whatever it takes to get Noah what he needs!

Above all just remember that your child is worth every single ounce of energy and time you invest in them. They can do anything as long as we prepare them!

Stephanie T., Noah's mom

Chapter 2
Person-Centered Planning

All our kids start out as cute little babies, dependent upon their own instincts and the caring guidance and protection of their parents or caregivers.

When our babies are born, we instantly become their lifeline—for food, for development, for all decision-making. Yet, we know they will all grow up in the years ahead. They will live and learn. They will experience life. Over the years, we entrust our children with more responsibilities until they typically become prepared to head off on their own in their late teens or early twenties. We all want our independence. It's a natural human drive. A recent study[8] showed personal happiness is most tied to autonomy—not money, material things, or even love, but autonomy.

However, for our kids and adults with Down syndrome, that process is often quite different. It's not really based on a specific time line or age because our self-advocates are unique. Some battle more serious medical conditions from birth than others. Some have greater physical or mental challenges than others. Like general society, people with Down syndrome span a rather wide spectrum. As parents, we discover these differences over time and seek to adjust our approach to guide their development. Often, this results in more hands-on direction for longer periods of time than for other kids.

This delayed development, along with our natural tendency to protect our most vulnerable, makes it even harder to gradually turn over the reins of decision-making every year. Yet, the post-high school "cliff" is not based on your child's development schedule but is forced upon us at a specific age, typically eighteen to twenty-two. Parents are often called upon to make essential decisions about education, day programs, work, and housing before they feel their self-advocate is ready to contribute to the discussion.

However, one mantra families with Down syndrome can attest: don't underestimate the talent and intellect of our loved ones. They will surprise you when you least expect it.

Getting to Know Them

Don't let the seemingly monotonous routines that our children with Down syndrome embrace mislead you. Many with Down syndrome are subtly expressive. But if we peel back the routines and superficial communication, we will find very bright, caring individuals with strong interests. We've discovered our daughter is an empath who, in turn, loves to be loved. She craves social acceptability and truly feels when others are sad or hurt. Gwendolyn is also very creative. She loves to make art and jewelry as much as she basks in the opportunity to sing and dance. These are important parts of her life and happiness.

Gwendolyn also has a keen desire for independence. She is quite observant, and she wants her life to look like those of her siblings, friends, and role models on TV. She wants to go to college, live on her own, and make her own decisions. Revealing these desires may take some pointed questions, keen observation, and a large dose of patience, but the value is tremendous in gaining insight about your self-advocate's dreams, as Gwendolyn exemplified when she populated her Independence Mind Map. Such discussions and mapping of thoughts, ideas, and aspirations is revealing and serves as a guidepost for your self-advocate's future.

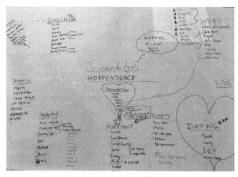

We are often surprised at Gwendolyn's ambitions and abilities. And Gwendolyn is certainly not alone. Most self-advocates crave independence. They don't want to be different. They want to be part of the community around them.

Our UPL Family Survey reveals:[9]

- 24 percent of our self-advocates want to attend college
- 65 percent want to work
- 47 percent desire to get married
- 50 percent aim to move out
- 31 percent hope to drive
- 44 percent enjoy travel

Larina, Camille's mother, says "she pushed us pretty hard to be human" while Fionn's dad, Jonathan, says Fionn is "embracing his Down syndrome and making the most of it" with their own production company and speaker's bureau. Finally, Chaya's mom, Thora, hears Chaya question, "If Down syndrome siblings can do it, why can't I?"

Parents often have the reasons why not, but our self-advocates embody the reasons why!

As many of us are already aware, our self-advocates are often indifferent to social norms. They may proudly wear creative mix-and-match outfits and sing or dance in bizarre places. They simply act based on what gives them joy. They see no obstacles in their way and they migrate toward people that believe in them. It is truly a freeing approach that makes them feel anything is possible. Far be it for us to squash that optimism.

Putting Them First

As parents and guardians, we may often get frustrated by the apparent limitations of the school system and its lack of foresight and confidence in our child's capabilities and ambitions. It is our responsibility to make sure we don't contribute to such cynicism but push back wherever it may reside. This prompts us to recognize the importance of having our self-advocate at the table so they can be part of their school Individualized Education Program (IEP), Admission, Review, Dismissal (ARD) process, and a long-term Independence Plan. We must remind ourselves to involve them in the very discussions and decisions that will frame their own lives.

In fact, they should not just be a figurehead at the table, but the star. They need to be engaged, to be asked their opinions and desires. If this doesn't flow freely, it is up to the parents, teachers, and others around them to spend the time to tap that input. **A plan without the star's understanding and buy-in is not truly a plan, but a directive.**

In the disabilities community, this is often referred to as person-centered planning (PCP), a movement whose motto is "nothing about us without us."[10] The Alzheimer's Disease & Down Syndrome Guidebook[11] provides seven principles of PCP:

1. To be acknowledged as a unique person
2. To feel loved and safe while being treated with respect
3. To be valued and included in their community
4. To be self-directed in decision-making to the greatest extent possible
5. To be involved in meaningful activity
6. To be provided comfort, care, and support with patience, compassion, and empathy
7. To have care that is focused on what individuals can do and not what they cannot do

It sounds so simple, yet we are apt to leave our self-advocates out of these processes. It is easier to make those decisions ourselves, but like everyone else, our self-advocates want to be heard. They want to be involved. Spend the time to teach them the process, ask the questions that will reveal their own interests, and use other approaches like alternative communication devices, pictures, drawings, or sign language. Implore teachers and others to make space for self-advocates in the discussion, and everyone will be amazed. It will empower the self-advocate while also making them accountable for the success of these decisions.

This does not mean the self-advocate should always get their way. None of us do. But it is critical they can voice their desires and opinions, that they can listen and participate in the debate about options, and that they understand the final decision. From this process, they recognize they are worthy. They are an important part of decisions about themselves and their lives. Fostering this involvement will help build the pride, decision-making skills, and confidence so critical for the independence of all our kids. It is no different for our self-advocates and their success on the road ahead. Our self-advocates are quite capable to participate in these discussions, but without this person-centered planning approach, the chances for the independence they seek is severely handicapped.

Aversion to Change—Evolution of Skills

Remember when your children were younger? It seemed that whenever we parents were completely exhausted and frustrated by a particular phase, our kids would move on to a new, exciting and praiseworthy stage. Perhaps this lingering is due to some subconscious reluctance to leave a perceived comfort zone or apprehension to enter a new, scary place. Regardless of whether this is an aversion to change or the evolution of skills and abilities, this is a natural occurrence. We all may require time to learn algebra or how to run a 5K, and also have to prepare ourselves for leaps into college, new work environments, or new relationships. This drive happens repeatedly in everyone's journey and the progression is necessary to continue to grow and develop to meet our personal goals.

It's no different for our kids with Down syndrome, albeit at a slower pace or more spread-out intervals than our other kids, but it happens. Frustration at the months of hands-on practice helping our loved one to crawl, walk, talk, or potty train often fades into the memory once they achieve these goals and move on to the next challenge. This progression provides parents with a sense of relief and hope, but it also offers our loved one confidence in their achievements and renewed focus for the next challenge ahead.

Navigating Plateaus

What happens to person-centered planning when the person at the center loses interest or stalls? Your independence plan must account for, and address, the reality of these plateaus.

Psychology Dictionary[12] **defines a plateau as "a time… whenever the learning curve flattens…frequently due to tiredness, boredom, loss of willingness, or a modification in the level of ability necessary."** These are all legitimate feelings for us and for our teen or adult with Down syndrome. They have the same human emotions as everyone else, after all. They may not figure out these feelings as easily or show or vocalize them in the same way, if at all. Hence, we may not even know they are in the midst of a developmental plateau.

Signs of plateauing to be aware of are:
- melancholia
- not being excited about favorite hobbies
- appearing lazy, sleepy, or otherwise out of sorts
- stopping or not performing common routines well
- reducing communication
- receiving remarks from teachers and friends that they don't seem themselves lately

Basically, any drastic change in behavior should be monitored.

How Can We Help?

Our loved ones may enjoy the routine, but **excessive repetition of the familiar breeds plateaus.** Creating flexibility and change throughout their growth will best prepare them for progress ahead. To curb the risk of plateaus, build a variety of activities, people, and places into their days. Plateaus are inevitable for us all, so developing the tools to manage such pauses will help our self-advocates get back on track more easily. When we identify a plateau, we can help our loved one progress through these steps:

1. Ask questions about their change in behavior.
2. Be supportive of their feelings.
3. Celebrate their recent successes.
4. Identify new mountains to climb, even if they are scary for them (and you).
5. Provide a gentler transition through modeling, practice, picture stories, checklists, and patience.
6. Seek ideas as well as alignment with your approach across the team (family, teachers, work managers, doctors, and therapists).
7. Talk about your own reluctance or fear with your spouse, your adult with Down syndrome, and a therapist. For us to be quality resources, we need to be on solid ground ourselves.

Independent Plateauing

Managing these plateaus as our self-advocates become more independent will continue to be challenging. Some people are better prepared to diagnose their feelings than others and some just have more energy and initiative than others. This can help them continue to push forward on their lifelong learning curve more than those who may need assistance and structure.

Create structure that includes encouragement and growth opportunities. Eventually, *any* job can become monotonous. Doing the same activities at a day program can become boring and lead to stagnation. If the expectation and prompting for continued growth does not exist, the conditions are ripe for stalling.

Solutions involve variety and change. Seek day programs that have a wide assortment of activities and people to socialize with every day. Ideally, some of these activities involve life skills and academics that will challenge your self-advocate to learn new materials and talents. Find vocational opportunities with caring managers who will teach and monitor your loved one, changing tasks and increasing responsibilities when appropriate. For those seeking independent housing, ensure the framework for continued growth is provided through independent activities like laundry, cooking, or other household tasks as well as the chance to progress from multiperson rooms to more independent suites or apartments.

Growth-centered structure and encouragement, along with their own experiences of change, will best prepare your self-advocate for lifelong learning. If they don't have such support, eventually a brief plateau may turn into extended stagnation or even regression, extinguishing the light we all adore on their face when they are full of pride from a new accomplishment.

Gwendolyn's Plateaus

Our daughter graduated high school in 2014. Gwendolyn enrolled in a full-time educational and social program for adults with Down syndrome immediately thereafter. That change provided her with the challenges and support she needed to move on from the high school plateau that formed during four years of the same people and learnings.

About two years later, we recognized her signals as she yearned for independence. We talked a lot to understand her specific desires and how we could support her dreams. We began working on skills (hygiene, cleaning, cooking, communications) to advance the cause.

Gwendolyn soon gained part-time employment to boost her skills and confidence and keep her challenged. A few years later, it seemed she was plateauing again. Even before the pandemic, she was sluggish at times. We determined she was ready for the next step in her Independence Plan.

Gwendolyn is now at a wonderful independent living community that supports her interests, but perhaps more importantly provides ongoing opportunities for growth, so that when plateaus arise, more challenges await.

The best way to identify those plateaus and to steer toward new challenges is to ensure your self-advocate is part of the process, that they have a say in how they feel and what they want. This involves inquiry and keen observation, which will help build your loved one's skills and ensure they remain "the most important part of [their] Independence Plan," as Gwendolyn emphatically states.

Sheila, who shares Dale's story below, admittedly has a unique parenting style. However, she is adamant that it has empowered Dale (age eighteen) to be independent as he continues to grow. Thus far, her approach has proven life changing.

Family Feature
Dale's Story

Empowered for Independence

In the 1990s I was an educator for adults with learning difficulties. I met loads of parents who couldn't imagine how their adult offspring would cope without them. In 2003 my newborn son, Dale, was diagnosed with Down syndrome—and eighteen years later the psychiatrist confirmed that he is also autistic.

Having met those parents of my students in the 1990s, I knew from the start the importance of planning to let go and to see my son managing without me. I'm not going to live forever. Losing one's parents is hard enough without having to cope with changes in daily routine as well.

I knew from my teaching experience that people with Down syndrome can learn very fast but find it very difficult to unlearn anything. I also knew the importance of positive language from my general life experience.

So, while Dale was learning to walk, aged two and a half, I taught him, "Stop at the curb." While my son was in his stroller or pushing his little trolley, we would always "Stop, look, listen" when we were walking along the sidewalk. By the time he could walk and run, aged three, he was always stopping at the curb. That had a huge benefit. It meant that Dale could run along the sidewalk, because I was absolutely confident that he wouldn't run into the road. He had no sense of danger or fear, but he always stopped at the curb. Later, I began to let him get off the bus one stop early and run that last block to school. I knew he would always stop at the curb. There were plenty of other families to cross the road with him. I could let him run free, because I had taught him to stay safe, strictly but without fear.

When Dale was about eight years old, we had a disagreement while out and about. I wanted to buy a newspaper but he wanted to go straight home. This was a journey we did every day. I reasoned that my son was not going to tell me I couldn't buy a newspaper, so I told him to take himself home: down the street, over a footbridge crossing a six-lane city highway, then two blocks to our house where an elder sibling was already home. I got home and was happy to find Dale had indeed taken himself home as expected.

Eventually we had a visit from local social services who were unhappy at the risks they felt I had been taking. They also accused me of allowing my son to go out with untidy clothes—I had encouraged him to dress himself without paying much attention to the finished result—and they said that I hadn't been feeding him properly. Believe me, once social services start on you, they will collect every story that might point to neglect or abuse. Of course, there are many cases of true abuse, but ours was merely an example of creative parenting.

I told them that yes, I'd taken risks, but I knew for certain that if I didn't allow Dale to take some risks then he would never get that vital sense of independence and would still be needing constant support at the age of thirty. If I taught him to stay close to me, it would be much harder to teach him to separate from me.

Now Dale is eighteen. I'm hoping we can soon get him living in his own studio apartment with support which will gradually reduce as he demonstrates his ability to manage on his own.

My son still can't understand risk, and I don't want to teach him any more fear. He's afraid of the dark and sleeps with his light on all night. He knows bad things sometimes happen. I reckon that my son will be motivated to be conscientious, by his desire to be seen as independent and competent. That's much more positive than fear.

Sheila, Dale's mom

SECTION II
FOSTERING INDEPENDENCE

Even with the proper mindset and vision, independence doesn't just happen. It takes a concerted effort from the earliest of ages to build strong habits and develop important skill sets. In this section, we first focus on developing skills and habits that will foster independence from an early age. Aids and ideas for making choices and building confidence will be presented in chapter 3.

Chapter 4 introduces the Social Circles Model to teach appropriate relationships for the wide range of people in your self-advocate's life. We will focus further on friendships and dating in order to boost self-esteem and camaraderie.

Communication is the focal point for chapter 5. Communication style and content support our loved one's journey. We will discuss how to meet them where they are and provide the tools for deeper interaction going forward.

Chapter 6 centers on safety and security, including steps to ensure safety in the house and tactics to enable their home alone time, as well as encouraging their independence out in the community.

Healthy hygiene habits, strong social skills, and safety awareness start early. Incorporating checklists, models, and training are critical in establishing routines, learning opportunities, and the self-confidence to foster independence at every stage.

If we start early, the transition from high school toward postsecondary programs, work, and independent living are just an extension of the journey the family has been on since birth.

Section II: Plans and Actions		
#	Action	Life Stage*
1	Download/customize your Daily Hygiene & Chores Checklist	Childhood
2	Create checklist for their home chores	Childhood
3	Download/populate your Social Circles Template	Childhood
4	Rectify home safety hazards	Childhood
5	Prepare and practice for "home alone"	Adolescence

If your loved one has passed this stage but has not completed this action, place this at the top of your action plan

Check out resources and references at the back of the book. Downloads are available for free at:

http://www.beyonddownsyndrome.net/The-Essential-Guide

Chapter 3
Building Blocks

What makes us independent? It's not just work or living on our own. It's our ability to make choices and decisions.

As kids, many of the choices and decisions affecting our lives were made by our parents. Eventually, we were on the road toward independence when we started making our own decisions. The first choice we made certainly couldn't be what kind of work we wanted to do or where we want to live. We had to start small—and early. We need to do the same for our future self-advocates.

Key building blocks of independence include:
- personal care
- chores
- hobbies

These building blocks develop skills and confidence in your self-advocate. With a mindset of future opportunities, not limitations, and a focus on person-centered planning, strive to introduce choices at the earliest stage.

Making Choices

It's best not to offer open-ended questions such as, "What do you want to eat today?" Rather start by providing options. "Cereal or yogurt? Water or juice? This shirt or that?" Give them time to decide. Educate them on the process—why might you choose one over another? Praise their decision-making process more so than the choice itself.

Suppose they choose a shirt and thirty minutes later wish they'd chosen a different shirt. Talk to them about why they may have changed their mind. Why didn't they choose the other shirt in the first place? Allow them to choose which shirt they want to wear now, perhaps leaving the other shirt for later in the day or the next. This experience is a great opportunity to help them understand choices and regrets while also empowering them to make personal decisions themselves.

If they are frustrated with the process and perhaps ask you to make the choice for them, resist. Talk about their frustrations and help them through the process but encourage them to make the decision themselves. When they are older, they will have many more decisions to make at school, at work, at social gatherings, and perhaps at their own place, and you will not be there. Now is the time to teach them the process, start to build their experience, and instill confidence in your self-advocate.

Creating Initiative

Beyond the primary goal of learning new skills, these activities also provide opportunities for them to **develop initiative and problem-solving skills, both critical components of independence.** They may understand how to make their bed or clean the dishes, but developing the initiative to do so without prompting, or at least without complaining and avoiding a tantrum, are valuable lessons. Furthermore, if they have loaded the dishwasher and pushed the "on" button but it doesn't turn on, they need the awareness to recognize something is wrong and either fix it or raise the issue to others. In the future, they will need to have these skills and the ability to raise their hand for help when they notice a problem.

Start with a job chart for everyone in the home so they see that everyone contributes to the family unit. Provide rewards and consequences around personal care and chores. Ask them how the activity went or if there were any problems or complications to discuss. You may even plant a problem and observe how they deal with it and then model how they can resolve it or tell others.

Our self-advocates are often creatures of habit, finding comfort in the familiar. Employing a wide variety of chores, hobbies, and field trips will help make such activities less structured and more pliable. That flexibility will prove quite helpful in the independent world of change and in busting through those inevitable plateaus to keep reaching for their dreams.

These building blocks are not just presented to foster independence for your self-advocate. They also help you, the supporting family member(s), gain confidence in your loved one's ability to handle a myriad of situations that will present themselves as they achieve greater independence, both at your home and beyond.

Personal Care

Ms. Smith, the life skills teacher at the Friends of Down Syndrome, remarks, "Some of [the students] don't dress themselves. They don't decide what they're going to put on, and I think that's a handicap. Let them put on what they want to put on and when they walk out that door and it's cold, then they'll know, I need to go put on something else or I need to do something different next time. Let them make some decisions…and then see how it works."

That approach can work well in providing some independence for selecting their outfit for the day, as well as for basic necessities that are essential for your loved one to master.

There are many items in this category that provide opportunities for practice throughout the day:

- Brush teeth
- Floss teeth
- Brush hair
- Get dressed
- Take a shower

These items can benefit from some initial show-and-tell. Don't assume they know how to do these tasks correctly. Talk to them about it. Show them. Observe, correct, monitor their attempts, and celebrate their efforts and successes.

Check in on them to not only make sure they've done the tasks, but just as importantly, that they are doing them correctly. Brushing for thirty seconds or avoiding shampooing their bangs for fear of getting soap in their eyes is not completing the task. Provide a checklist to remind them when these tasks should be done every day. You can use pictures or symbols as well as words to boost their reading skills. Celebrate progress starting with initial task completion and continuing until each becomes a habit.

Good habits are with them for life; bad habits are very hard to break. Our loved ones tend to be much more pliable as toddlers and considerably more resistant as teens and adults. Besides, teaching a teen to brush their teeth or wipe well after going to the bathroom is tiresome for the parent, frustrating for the teen, and frankly extraordinarily difficult after years of neglect. These critical tasks help avoid infections and social embarrassment.

Start to transition these activities as early as possible. This will also ease a transition into further items like shaving and managing their menstrual cycle. These tasks are the first on the road to independence, so they create the mindset that not only will you, the parent, not be brushing their teeth and bathing them forever, but that they must learn to do important activities themselves.

We will cover more health-related items include nutrition, fitness, and common health issues for adults with Down syndrome in chapter 7.

Household Chores

Teaching our loved one new chores does take some investment. It is not so easy as to merely invite them to wash the dishes, make their bed, do a load of laundry, or take out the trash and know it will get done. Honestly, it's not that simple for *any* of our kids, especially if you want the job done correctly and on schedule.

For our self-advocates, teaching chores requires planning in five steps:

1. Model the chore: Invite them to observe you doing the task in a slow and deliberate fashion.
2. Teach the steps: Instruct them step-by-step and let them practice each.
3. Provide a checklist: Use a list and pictures to illustrate each step so they can perform the task on their own.
4. Oversee and manage: Observe them doing the chore and make adjustments to their process and the checklist as necessary.
5. Lavish with praise: Build up their ego with earned praise.

Through these steps, they will become contributing members of the household, responsible for certain tasks important to your family. With completion of the fifth step, they will be prepared to take on more tasks. Not only does this help get household chores done and build their confidence, but it prepares them for the day they may live in their own home and need to do these tasks without prompts or assistance.

Teachable chores can be practically anything around the house. Some tasks are more complex than others, so start simple and with the ones your self-advocate is most interested in. Many of our feature families have listed these:

Making the bed	Cleaning their room
Setting the table	Clearing the table
Wiping kitchen counters	Cleaning bathrooms
Vacuuming	Mopping/sweeping
Taking out garbage/recycling	Gardening
Feeding pets	Taking pets for a walk
Loading/unloading dishwasher	Putting dishes away
Prepping meals	Cooking in microwave/on stovetop
Washing/drying laundry	Putting clothes away

Let's look at a sample step-by-step process for doing the laundry:

1. Sort laundry into whites, darks, bright colors, towels, and sheets
2. Washing
   a. Put clothes in the washer up to the lowest rim

b. Measure detergent to line "2" of the bottle top and pour into the top front triangle

c. Measure softener to top rim of the bottle top and pour into back right triangle

d. Close door

e. Turn knob:

Clothes	**Knob light**
Whites	Whites
Darks	Normal
Brights	Colors
Towels	Bulky
Sheets	Sheets

f. Press POWER

g. All done! Good job!

Take a picture of your washer and mark or draw arrows to the containers, knobs, or buttons. Use this list and pictures every time you do the laundry with your self-advocate so they understand the process and can lean on the list as they learn to do laundry themselves. Once you've run through the steps many times and made any adjustments, laminate the process list and keep it by the washer for easy access. This may seem complicated at first but following the steps above will help your loved one master this chore.

It is always easier to develop these skills from early childhood than when they are suddenly anxious to have their independence in their twenties or beyond.

Dale, who we met in the last chapter, tidies his room and cooks a bit, too. Sheila ensures he does at least one chore every day after school. Ethan, who we will meet later, makes his bed, hangs his clothes to dry, puts them away, sets the table, and puts laundry in the hamper. Amanda, who you will meet in one of our **Family Features** at the end of this chapter, sweeps the house, does her own laundry, and has learned to cook in the kitchen. Ayla's mom, Heather, developed a jobs board in which her kids get points and eventually prizes when they complete assigned tasks like walking the dogs, recycling, and cleaning the counter, with extra points for helping with something not on their list.

Art, Noah's dad, reminds us that caring for pets provides an excellent role model for our self-advocates. Pets are typically highly dependent on the caregiver and provide feedback when they are satisfied or needy. Consider making your loved one the primary caregiver of a family pet.

Proactively building these skill sets contributes to a smoother transition toward greater independence.

Hobbies

Exploring hobbies is important for all of us. With positive support, hobbies encourage curiosity toward discovering interests and creating new skills as well. Some hobbies may develop your loved one's dexterity or athleticism; others may help them learn about themselves and how to socialize with others. Seek out these opportunities with your self-advocate. Give them a long list of options. Ask them what they are most interested in. Support their exploration as well as their choice to continue some and end others. As with all kids, **this early stage is a breeding ground for near-term happiness and lifelong passions.** These hobbies may become sources of common social interactions as well as job prospects in the future. Dancing and singing may lead to self-advocates circling local dances on their schedule or concert events on their calendar. Listening to music may lead to surfing the internet to learn more about their favorite artists. Computer skills and confidence may evolve into administrative jobs. Helping to prepare meals at home can lead to a food-prep job at a local restaurant. And what's most amazing of all is when these become passions, they provide bright spots in their day and heightened self-confidence in their specialty. Imagine the possibilities.

Hobbies may also help tackle common health issues. Exposing your child to a wide variety of sports with the family, at school, and through Special Olympics will help them burn calories and invigorate their metabolism.

Amanda is an artist who has created her own company, "Amanda's Art with Heart" where she makes notecards from her paintings. She also likes photography and archery. Daniel enjoys classes at his local recreation center along with bingo, bowling, miniature golf, and church bible study. Ayla and Slayton, who are **Family Features** at the end of this chapter, thrive at Special Olympics, cooking, and woodwork.

Here is a brief list of hobbies to consider:

Music & singing	Dancing
Reading	Writing
Special Olympics	Walking/biking
Tennis	Basketball

Bowling	Swimming
Art	Jewelry making
Woodwork	Archery
Video games	Online learning
Theatre	Sewing
Coloring	Puzzles

Don't limit your hobby search to "special needs-only" activities. Let their interests guide you. Seek a variety of groups. Find those that have an open heart and see the benefit to all that participate when your son or daughter joins in. Not only will this become the basis for skills and confidence, but as social interaction increases you will find special people that may be in your life forever. Such angels give of their time, connect with your loved one through some unspoken bond, and shine a light upon you and your family. These are the silver linings of hobbies and connections. As the lead advisor of your self-advocate's team, you have a great opportunity to cultivate ideas and opportunities for their lifelong development. Hobbies are a great place to start.

Field Trips

Building blocks for independence are all around you, not just at home. Field trips to restaurants, groceries, and other outings provide great opportunities for learning and skills development.

Restaurants offer a chance to practice table manners and discuss nutrition and healthy options. These outings can also boost your self-advocate's confidence. Let them review the menu, ask questions, and select and order their choice. It provides empowerment and pride. Gwendolyn's face beamed when she first ordered a meal herself. Then, she couldn't stop reminding us that she ordered "all by myself." If your loved one is not yet a reader, there are many restaurants with pictures on their menu to assist. Don't miss these opportunities by selecting and ordering for your loved one.

The grocery store is another fertile place for learning. Build your shopping list together at home. At the grocery, show them how you evaluate options for peanut butter and detergent as you check off the list. They will begin to notice nutritional labels and price points. Help them understand the layout of the store and when you might engage with store staff or even say a casual hello to fellow shoppers. Finally, offer your self-advocate the opportunity to do a bit of shopping of their own. Give them part of your shopping list or let them make their own. They may start out with ten items and their own shopping cart, perhaps looking on one aisle for the items. Eventually, give them a longer list and a budget which they can track with their smart phone calculator. You may choose to wait at the front of the store or to sneak behind them to check on their progress. What a great way for them to learn and build self-confidence. Granted, they may select more temptations off their list than what's actually *on* their list, as Gwendolyn often does, but the experience is everlasting.

Finally, consider other field trips such as museums, libraries, shopping malls, parks, camping, and public transportation. Each provides a chance for learning and independence. All self-advocates aspire to be out in the world, blending in with the general public. These field trips give them chances to develop and practice skills navigating signs, seeing how other people conduct themselves, and broadening their horizons.

Focus Through Smart Phones

Smart phones and technology have become both the "great enabler" and the "bane of our existence." We may often struggle in deciding when (no longer "if") to expose any of our kids to this life-changing experience. While smart phones do present challenges, they also contain a bevy of learning opportunities. Your loved one will learn how to talk on the phone, but even more, how to use apps like the calculator, calendar, and alarm. These can be of great assistance when they are shopping (calculator) and preparing for their day (calendar). Smart phones can remind them of important obligations including taking pills, taking a shower, or when to go to a program or event (alarm). Along with these valuable tools, mobile phones offer the chance to talk about the dangers around security and social interaction, both of which we will cover in subsequent chapters. You may also install safeguards on their phone to limit their calls, their time on social media, the sites they may visit, and their ability to make purchases. So smart phones become a fantastic learning ground as well as a chance to teach about the risks of the world around them in a relatively safe environment. I would encourage you to consider providing your self-advocate with their own phone at the same age as their siblings.

Joyce, Amanda's mom, shares an inspiring story of the active lifestyle Amanda lives through helping and hobbies while Stacy Lynn describes Slayton's ambitious approach to life and learning.

Family Feature
Amanda's Story

From the day Amanda was born, she was fighting for her life, her breath, and her independence. She was born in Germany on her due date, but not without complications. After being resuscitated, she was swiftly put in the NICU, where she had to be independent of me. Twenty-five years later, she continues working toward that independence and control in her life.

We realized that every day was a lesson, from gaining strength in her fingers so she could tie her shoes to ultimately sorting her laundry. Did this make sense when she was a toddler? Not really, but sometimes you can't see things unfold until they are right there in front of you.

Surfer Girl

Amanda has an excellent memory and an insatiable curiosity. We find that working with her strengths creates a solid foundation for skills that foster independence. She likes to know "why" and what we will do tomorrow or Monday and Tuesday, and what about Wednesday? We've taught her how to use the calendar on her phone to know when her appointments are, which satisfies her curiosity. She loves to surf the internet for her favorite actors, singers, and movies. We monitor her internet viewing through open communication. We've had several discussions about unapproved purchases and what she views, and she does not have any social media accounts. Mistakes happen, and this is the way we learn.

Learning Through Helping

Amanda likes to help people. When she was about eight, she saw her friend Danny working at the local grocery store and asked what he was doing. I told her he was helping us with our groceries. So, to this day, when we go shopping, Amanda helps me with the groceries, from the cart to the car, and organizing the pantry. This is a natural thing for her to do. She started helping in the kitchen this way by asking, "Do you need any help?" So, of course, I put her to work. She will often ask if the dishes are clean or dirty. Some days she might not feel like assisting. I will prompt her by saying it will really "help" me, which seems to be the key word.

Amanda helps me dust and sweep the floor. She also does her own laundry. She will fold her clothes and put them away. She prefers to hang her T-shirts up while I stuff mine in a drawer. She's a very snappy dresser and lays out her clothes the night before. Regardless of what I'm doing, if I'm painting a room or washing my motorcycle, Amanda is ready to pitch in.

My mother taught Amanda how to cook. I've kept this up when we cook on the weekends. She can prep food, wash vegetables, cut them, oil the pan, and stir-fry. During the week, Amanda gets organic, freshly cooked meals that she warms up by herself. We input the meals into a program on the computer that keeps track of her calorie intake. We talk about her nutrition and weight a lot; she has lost over twenty pounds.

Endless Hobbies

Amanda is an artist and volunteered at a local museum, but when the pandemic closed the museums, she started her own business. "Amanda's Art with Heart" was created to spread her artwork in the form of note cards. We sold them at art craft fairs and had some at a local store in the mall. Besides painting, Amanda is an excellent archer with an array of professional-grade bows and arrows. She is also a Special Olympic gold and silver medalist in swimming and track and field. She has tried Tai Chi, sailing, and white-water river rafting and traveled all over Europe, the Caribbean, Canada, and the United States.

Throughout Amanda's life, we have strived to give her opportunities and responsibilities, both of which have fostered her independence as a lovely young lady.

Joyce, Amanda's mom

Family Feature
Slayton's Story

Little By Little

Slayton is a kind, strong, well-adjusted sixteen-year-old now, but what a jellyfish, wreck of a baby he was! I wondered at times if he had any muscles under that skin and if he'd ever roll over, sit up, or even swallow his food by himself. However, he was spunky and strong-willed, and I was determined to help him! After all, adversity is the breeding ground for success, right?

Slayton lives with me, his mama, his stepfather Rick, and his younger brother Julian, who is fifteen. The two boys are homeschooled, and we are tightly knit. Early on, I chose to do his PT and OT and trained him in just about all skills. Chores and projects have been my choice of teaching since the early days. So many skills can be gained by retrieving items, maneuvering a broom and dustpan, filing folders, and following multistep instructions. These are not only building his skill sets for the future, but also are boosting his self-esteem. My dad always said, "The more things you know how to do, the more options you have." Slayton needs as many options as possible.

Chores Develop Skills

As Slayton has gotten older and more proficient in the chores he does, I have expanded his training to the outdoors. Raising three boys (the other is now twenty-seven), dirt, woods, and hard, sweaty work are a natural part of life. Chores and tasks are chosen based on the skills Slayton still needs to develop. Two years ago, for instance, I decided we needed to carve a garden out of our bushy backyard. This involved clearing brush, digging roots, securing fencing to bamboo poles, digging mounds of earth, tilling, and building garden boxes assembled from pallet wood. We even built a large fort seven feet off the ground in between growing seasons! Slayton helped with every aspect of these projects.

It sounds so simple when written in these short sentences, but this was a two-year-long process. Like everything taught to Slayton before this, every skill had to be broken up into smaller chunks and done with a lot of repetition. For instance, it took fifteen minutes for Slayton to maneuver the drill chuck and secure it into place, and even longer to push the drill against the pole, while pulling the pole toward the drill so the screw would go into the pole. Spending this much time on one single little skill seems irrational by most standards—and it certainly feels that way in process. But he must learn to do all he can for himself in order to fulfill the level of independence we want for him, and that he wants for himself.

Hobbies Develop Passions

Slayton has developed some passions that foster performance and pride. Slayton LOVES playing the drums. It's one of his favorite hobbies, and he plays well. He also tap dances with typical students at a large dance studio. Not bad for a boy who still can't clap to a tempo and struggled for years to skip and pedal a bike. If we ever need something done methodically with a shovel, Slayton is the first one we call!

He was the preferred digger when we put in our small orchard this past spring because his holes were so perfectly shaped. He can do all of his self-care activities, with some tweaking of his collar, a cuff, and the fixing of an occasional rogue hairdo. These accomplishments are encouraging because they remind us that he CAN and (eventually) will succeed in whatever he sets his mind to.

Slayton's Future Is Bright

Although Slayton is capable in many areas now, he still has a long way to go toward independence. We are currently working on how he interacts with his peers and what appropriate behavior looks like in different situations using role-play. He still isn't as aware of his surroundings as he needs to be, like when he's walking in a parking lot near moving cars or near the street. We are beginning to practice doing job interviews, and transactions at the store and online. Slayton doesn't have a solid understanding of money and its value, so this will take some work. He is wanting a "real" job, so how to fill out an application is going onto our "to learn" roster. For now, he is pacified by doing small jobs for friends or family and getting paid, which he likes.

Little by little we inch forward. I don't know what the end result will look like, but there are a couple of things I do know for sure. One is that ready or not, Slayton was given to me, not some other mom. I must be the one best equipped to help prepare him, even if I don't always feel I am, so I will exhaust my efforts to help him. The second certainty is that with God, all things are possible, and I trust that He will make up the difference.

Stacy Lynn, Slayton's mom

Chapter 4
Social Circles & Relationships

This chapter is near and dear to my heart. It captures both our greatest hopes and fears as parents.

From the moment of their birth, we simply hope our kids are happy and know love. Yet we sense that our children's warmth and needs can be accompanied by a degree of naivete that makes them vulnerable to bad elements that unfortunately exist in every community. How can we help our self-advocates know the difference?

First, let's step back and celebrate their personality and reclassify their "naivete." Most in the Down syndrome community are indeed less aware of their surroundings, and while that creates some vulnerabilities, it is a learning opportunity for all of us. They don't worry about social standards—whether regarding dress, appearance, or behavior.

Especially as a kid, Gwendolyn always had her unique way of mixing and matching stripes and patterns. She loved her music and often danced and sang with headphones on while walking in the mall or waiting in the airport. I think this is a beautiful thing. I've always felt there is so much I can learn from Gwendolyn, and her disinterest in societal norms is tops on the list. True, she isn't really aware of those norms, but that is the point. Perhaps the rest of us just spend too much time trying to be well-versed in these norms and making sure we don't stray too far from them lest we attract unwanted attention. Most self-advocates don't give that a second thought. What a wonderful gift they offer us in these moments.

Yet, it is true, others may use our self-advocates' openness and innocence to do harm. Pickpockets are everywhere and serious crime happens every day around the world. As adults, we have learned to be extra vigilant but not to extract ourselves from the world around us. We need to teach and allow our self-advocates to do the same. That starts with a discussion of relationships using the Social Circles Model. **This simple model can aid in discussions with your self-advocate about who fits in each category and what is appropriate and inappropriate regarding sharing, talking, and touching for each group.**

Katie Thune, president and founder of Mad Hatter Wellness, LLC, which seeks to educate, train, and empower people with intellectual disabilities and their support systems, suggests all engagements should include healthy boundaries and consent. In all cases, if someone wishes to hold hands, hug, or kiss your self-advocate, they should ask, wait for a response, and respect the choice made. This obviously applies to strangers, but it also applies to friends and family. In different moments or moods, your loved one may feel more or less comfortable engaging with others, including any form of embrace. That is their right. Boundaries and consent promote self-respect, their ability to say no, and the importance of protecting their own space. The Social Circles Model will prove a handy reference for your self-advocate for years to come.

THE SOCIAL CIRCLES MODEL

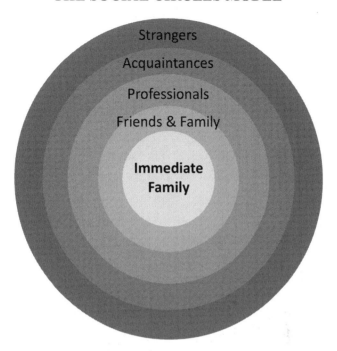

Immediate Family: By definition, these are trusted, close family members—typically parents and siblings, perhaps extending to grandparents, aunts, or uncles. These are the people that know, love, and accept your self-advocate for who they are. There is a high degree of trust and sharing of thoughts and confidential information within this group. Hugs and kisses can be appropriate. This category represents the core of the Independence Team and could be involved in their daily monitoring and support, but definitely should be part of the longer-term Independence Plan development and execution. This group may be one person—or a half dozen. Each member should know they are part of this group and enthusiastically want to participate in all that this group entails. *Keywords: close, trusting, hugs with consent*

Friends and Family: This group includes extended but well-known family along with close friends. They provide sounding boards, social skills development opportunities, and friendship. They may be close, but you want to know if your self-advocate is spending time with these people. Schedule the playdates and be aware of what they are doing. They certainly should care for the best interest of your child, but they are likely not as well-versed on all the nuances of Down syndrome. Family should be trained on how to support independence while also monitoring outside risks in public. Friends may include others with Down syndrome or other disabilities, as well as mainstream neurotypicals. This is their social circle of friends and is quite important. However, they are slightly removed from the most intimate levels of trust and touch. Hugs and hand holding may be appropriate but further contact is not. *Keywords: friends, sharing, playdates, hand holding with consent*

Professionals: This category includes teachers, doctors, and therapists. It is important that the parent or caregiver has established a relationship with these people. You should share expectations of service and your person-centered planning approach so they may include the same in their interaction. For example, the doctor should talk with and to your self-advocate, not around them to you. They should ask your self-advocate what they want, how they feel, and why they feel that way. This category should be role appropriate. Your doctor should be trusted with information regarding your loved one's health and well-being and be able to examine your self-advocate in an appropriate way. Obviously, teachers would not have that same access, but you want your self-advocate to feel comfortable talking with them about their interests and frustrations in order to pursue an appropriate development plan. It's important to explain these differences to your self-advocate so they know how best to engage with each professional. Some members of this group may also be part of the Independence Team, albeit perhaps as consultants. Handshakes can be appropriate for this category. *Keywords: teacher, doctor, sharing information, handshakes with consent*

Acquaintances: This category includes schoolmates, coworkers, and even relatives that your self-advocate has met but does not know well. However, these are not close friends and are not considered to be in the circle of trust. It is fine to talk to these people and waves or handshakes are appropriate. These are likely not people your self-advocate would be left alone with unless within a structured group setting like school or work. People may move from this category to the friends and family circle and even vice versa. This can be a confusing category because they are neither strangers nor close friends so describing the group concept and role modeling it yourself (pointing out who is in this circle for you) is helpful. *Keywords: hello, cautious, buddy system, waves*

Strangers: This group seems obvious. These are people who your self-advocate doesn't know. They could be friends or acquaintances of yours but new to them, in which case you can introduce them, but they still may remain strangers to your self-advocate. Amanda's mom, Joyce, shares, "Amanda is a magnet for strangers because they just want to come up to her and hug her and tell me how beautiful she is." While we aspire for our loved one's inclusion in society, generally, I would advise our kids to avoid strangers unless there is someone else with them to make introductions, in which case a handshake and general conversation may be appropriate. Otherwise, I'd rather guide our self-advocates not talk to strangers, not to shake hands with strangers, and of course, never to walk with or get into cars with strangers. This may be a scary discussion for you and your loved one, but it is necessary to ensure they do understand the risks that are out there. It is part of a full and balanced discussion of the Social Circles Model, so they are neither too scared to talk to anyone nor too comfortable to hug everyone. ***Keywords: stay away, avoid, caution***

Use our downloadable worksheet or make your own spreadsheet or notebook to classify people into each category with keywords at the top of each group as a handy reminder. Post the list in your self-advocate's room. Update and discuss it periodically.

Friendships

Friendships can be tricky for our self-advocates, but they are essential in building a sense of camaraderie and elevating self-esteem and mental health. Friendships help our loved ones share feelings and fears, have a trusted sounding board for ideas, and gain a sense of community. By relating to others, people don't feel alone or wonder what is commonplace or acceptable and what might be strange. Often, our self-advocate's friendships tend to appear superficial, filled with general chitchat and funny antics without much depth or body, yet they do provide warmth to our loved ones. It can be hard for them to establish deeper conversations on their own. Offer to host a playdate or take them out for lunch to help get the conversation going. Ask questions about their background and interests so they will recognize what they have in common. Promote follow-up conversations and ask your loved one what they are learning about their closest companions and how they are doing.

Daniel's mom, Carolyn, got creative: "We started a sort of friendship club. We had six young adults with Down syndrome, and we met once a week. The young adults decided on what they wanted to do. Each week one parent would help facilitate the activity chosen by the group and provide transportation. That way the other parents got an afternoon or evening off and this enabled the friends to be more independent during the activity. It is a great way to make friends as sometimes they need structure and activity to help them relate."

Katie Thune of Mad Hatter Wellness[14] suggests good friendships involve sharing, taking turns, respecting boundaries, and compromising. However, as with any group of friends, drama can ensue. Ms. Smith of the Friends of Down Syndrome has seen feelings hurt by unintended nudges or smirks, or people not sitting next to others at lunch. She reminds her students that everyone has a bad day sometimes and not everyone will be friends with others. She tells them, "Don't let anybody else control your day. They don't decide what kind of day you're gonna have. It's gonna be a good day if you say it is. I say 'kick rocks'—don't worry about it and move on. You cannot be friends with everybody all the time. Go find somebody else to be your friend today."

Drama can go with the territory, but the value of friendships is paramount. Depression and feelings of loneliness are prevalent among adults with disabilities. We all need someone to share our innermost thoughts with so they don't just stew in our heads. Help your self-advocate cultivate those relationships.

Dating and Sex

We should not be surprised that our teen self-advocates develop feelings and even urges. This is as normal for them as it is for us. They may not understand them any better than we did when we were their age.

You can help by talking about the difference between friend and boyfriend/girlfriend. As Ms. Smith of the Friends of Down Syndrome notes, "They all want to be loved and liked. Some of them don't know the difference between the two." I presume that most boyfriend/girlfriend relationships start as friends, and perhaps best friends, before possibly advancing to a warmer relationship. In such bonds, they want to share secrets with each other and spend more time talking and playing together. Then you may expect the topic of "mutual attraction" to be introduced. Dating relationships are based on both people having similar interests and attractions—otherwise it's just a crush from afar. Encourage them to talk about their feelings with you and with each other. Support and shuttle them for dinners, movies, and playdates so they can explore their relationship. Keep an eye out for hand holding and consider providing them some private time for kissing, if/when the relationship has advanced.

Many parents are understandably nervous about this big step. I encourage you to coordinate these developments with the other person's parents. Try having the parents and self-advocates out for dinner to talk and to observe the self-advocates at a separate table. This might help soften reluctant parents and promote a happy relationship for everyone. If the other parents are not supportive of their loved one dating or kissing, you will need to have a conversation with your self-advocate to reframe the relationship and should encourage the other parents to do the same. Misalignment often doesn't end well, leaving the self-advocates frustrated and confused. Discouraging or forbidding such relationships is not healthy. It's denying your loved one their most basic instinct and desire for close friendships. It's better to support these relationships with a dose of caution and a watchful eye.

I would also encourage you to consider a "birds-and-bees" conversation with your self-advocate. It doesn't matter whether they are a boy or girl. It's the same as with our other kids. It can be an awkward and uncomfortable conversation for everyone, but I'd rather them hear it from me than perhaps a distorted (or perverted) version of the truth from other "friends," TV, the internet, or a stranger. This doesn't have to be graphic, but having a candid, adult conversation with proper words for body parts is usually appropriate. This is a good time to reiterate the concept of consent. Both people should know that mutual respect is essential and that "no" means no—to anything. They should also understand that kissing is for girlfriends/boyfriends and touching privates is for people that are either in an advanced relationship or married, depending on your personal view. This may not be your true moral position, or mine, but given the concept and free flowing expressions of "love," if you just say touching is for those in love, you may introduce confusion or advanced issues much earlier than you'd like.

You may also run into the conversation of babies with your son or daughter. This is a natural ambition for adolescents, but given it is very unlikely people with Down syndrome can conceive and even more unlikely they will be in a position to care for a baby, we opted to nix this idea early on. It can be confusing and heartbreaking, but it is better than them continuing to develop that vision in their head when it is one of the things that is just not feasible.

Finally, I will gingerly approach the topic of self-pleasure. Your views and openness to discussions with any of your kids is a personal choice. Specifically for your self-advocate, including this in your discussions can help them understand what otherwise may feel awkward or shameful. If you had a conversation with any of your kids, then be prepared to have a similar conversation with your self-advocate. Otherwise, at least make space for them to do their own exploring. Institute privacy rules in the house, ask them if they have any questions as their body changes, and be supportive. This is a confusing time for any teens and young adults. Let's try not to make it more confusing by leaving our self-advocates to figure out these feelings on their own.

At a 2020 National Down Syndrome Society (NDSS) Virtual Adult Summit, a panel of self-advocates tackled these issues. Four themes emerged:

1. Self-advocates are adults and should have information from parents about relationships and intimacy.
2. They have the same needs and desires as everyone else.
3. Open communication of interests and limits should be shared by both people.
4. Parents and caregivers should be kind and caring, but overprotection may deprive self-advocates of the spice of life.[15]

Clearly, resistance to discussions or support doesn't stop the interest, just the communication.

Relationships are the backbone of society and of who we are. Developing close, trusting friendships is imperative for all of us, whether with one person or many. We need to help our self-advocates understand what is appropriate and how they can manage the wide variety of relationships they encounter every day.

Social Options

Throughout their lives your self-advocate will want playdates and social interaction, whether they can express that or not. Talk to your self-advocate about their interests. Run these options by them and try a few at a time:

- Special Olympics: This is a great way to combine fitness, social interaction, and confidence building.
- Dance parties: Find them through your local Down syndrome association or school.
- Local social groups: There are a variety of groups to choose from, including parent-organized groups and scheduled programming such as through GiGi's Playhouse. Discover further options through your local Down syndrome association or the internet.
- Summer camps: There are many Down syndrome and special needs camps. You can consider inclusive camps, but you might find interests and abilities diverge as kids get older. Your child may become less comfortable with inclusive camps with their age group by the time they are teens.
- Best buddies programs: These provide inclusive opportunities for playdates, friendships, and skills building.
- Day programs: After high school, the right program offers both the educational and social development your self-advocate craves.
- State and national conventions: There are several conventions, including the National Down Syndrome Society (NDSS) and National Down Syndrome Congress (NDSC) that provide valuable information for parents along with informative and social tracks for attending self-advocates.
- Advocacy programs: More self-aware people with Down syndrome may develop an interest to advocate for themselves

and others with Down syndrome or other I/DD. There are many opportunities through The Arc, Easterseals, NDSS, NDSC, and others to advocate within the community or within local/state/national legislatures. This is a great way to build interest and self-confidence for those that are inclined.

There are many other ways to expose your self-advocate to social opportunities. Start by discussing these options, as well as their hobbies and interests, to find choices they are drawn to. Consider what you enjoy and invite them along. Joyce and her daughter Amanda love going to a "sip and paint" events, and Gwendolyn is thrilled to go to concerts or other music venues.

I also want to remind everyone that while our loved ones have a third twenty-first chromosome in common, they are all different. Some are more extroverted, thus craving more social contact, while others are more introverted. That doesn't mean they don't enjoy playdates or fun outings; they just may need some help to get started and usually will prefer to engage with small groups for a shorter period of time before they need to re-energize with some alone time.[16]

In the story below, mom, Larina, comments, "I want Camille to have skills to integrate, to shop, to go to church. As vital as independence is, it is also important to have interdependence." Camille's story of her social successes and challenges is this chapter's **Family Feature**.

Family Feature
Camille's Story

Brian and I live in Davidson, a vibrant college town just north of Charlotte, North Carolina, with our daughters: Camille (who is fourteen and has Down syndrome) and Nora (eleven).

One of Camille's strengths is her ability to carry on a conversation with ease, which has opened the door for many meaningful relationships in her life. Her speech itself is fluid and mostly intelligible, which I honestly attribute to luck. However, we do have to support her social skills at every turn. In other words, while our young lady has the gift of gab, this doesn't mean that socializing—literally, interacting with other people—has always been comfortable or obvious to her.

To satisfy her need and desire for social interaction, we let Camille use FaceTime to connect with friends and family. She enjoys seeing faces while having a conversation. Summers can be lonely at times because she doesn't do well at camp—it's too new and overwhelming. I haven't found an alternative, even with childcare support, that allows her to socialize adequately in the summer; we just do our best to create a "potpourri life" of her favorite activities and that gets us all through.

In Camille's homeschool co-op, her goals include working on introductions ("Hi, I'm Camille. It's nice to meet you!"); ordering food at restaurants (by looking at the server instead of mumbling about what she wants to eat); greeting people and saying "goodbye" or "have a nice day" at the appropriate times (instead of skipping over simple politeness!); and using check-in questions such as "How was school, Nora?" or "Mom, did you have a good time with your friends?" which not only show good manners, but also paves the way for actual conversations. In giving her the language tools, we are also building her confidence: each time she has a successful interaction with someone, it makes it a little easier the next time.

We practice social skills because we have to. Camille is very friendly and enjoys interacting with people she knows but the game totally changes when she has to interact with strangers (which is part of life whether we like it or not). Despite her comfort with conversation, we rarely have a concern about her safety. Honestly, I don't really have her out of my sight and when she is, she's with someone I trust implicitly.

Camille has friends across the life span. Same-age peers are the hardest match because, developmentally, Camille does not track at the biological age of her peers. Young children and older teens do very well with her; middle schoolers (where we are now) can be a little tricky. Those who don't pay much attention to the Down syndrome piece and who just go straight to enjoying her company create the best relationships; thankfully, there are many of these folks in her life.

Our top relationship challenge right now is that Camille would love to have more friends her age. If anything makes me sad as a parent in this season, it's that this doesn't happen organically. I try to focus my energy on the people in her life who love her and "get" her, inviting them into our home and her world as often as possible to foster her sense of belonging and connectedness. As for same-age peers, friendships just can't be forced. At most, I might ask a willing parent to support their child's involvement in Camille's life, but I haven't found the ultimate solution. Many of my friends in the Down syndrome community seem to be in the same boat with their teenagers. Camille is a wonderful friend—she cares about what you care about and remembers what matters to you. Hopefully, in time, she will add more friends in her age group.

Somewhat ironically, Camille struggles with individuals in the disability community. She is more at ease with people without speech or behavioral challenges. I was not expecting this, but it does make sense now that I know her. Camille needs people who can handle her, who can initiate conversations and activities, and who can sustain the relationship regardless of what she's doing. She is very dear to so many people and despite everything that feels hard about raising her, she is the center of my heart, and we appreciate all that she brings to this world.

Larina, Camille's mom

Chapter 5
Communications

Everyone communicates. Even trees "talk" to each other through their roots, odors, and offspring,[17] sharing their needs and wants in a collaborative effort to survive and thrive. Trees lean away from some others to get the sunlight they need and intertwine root systems to cooperate with others that are vital to their existence. In much the same way, our self-advocates lean toward communications and work with others through their own communication roots to obtain the support they need. Through communication, they share their fears and anxieties and their hopes and dreams. They also convey their understanding, apprehension, or confusion about a situation, request, or requirement.

For many, such sharing involves a long evolution of speaking skills, and for others it is largely nonverbal, but communication, nonetheless. Our self-advocates represent a broad spectrum of communication styles. Respondents to our UPL Family Survey indicated 86 percent are verbal, 30 percent write, and 13 percent utilize sign language.[18] Many others may use visual cues or augmented alternative communication (AAC) technologies. We just have to open our minds to such diverse ways of communicating.

Meet Them Where They Are

Communication styles evolve over time. Our role is first to meet them where they are. If they are nonverbal, we must strive to understand their needs and share our expectations in a way that they will understand. Many behavioral problems stem from a lack of communication.[19] Taking the time to truly engage makes a tangible difference in everyone's life.

Communication is a two-way street. It requires someone to express thoughts, feelings, or needs and another to listen and respond. In addition to a degree of skills required by both participants, the rapport between the two is critical. Most of our self-advocates seem to have an intuitive sense when it comes to establishing relationships. They can tell who is genuinely interested in them and comfortable to play and converse while shunning others who appear to just be going through the motions. One of Gwendolyn's first speech therapists called us after several sessions at school. She regretted to inform us that she feared Gwendolyn may never be verbal. My wife and I looked at each other and smirked. Even at that young age, Gwendolyn could talk up a storm at home. She often replicated the day's classroom sessions at home with her dolls. We had to break it to the therapist that she was quite verbal, but unfortunately, she didn't yet feel that chemistry with the therapist. Finding such connections can be life changing.

In 2005, our family moved from Texas to London on a work transfer. The change was intense for all of us. We adjusted to new rules and customs in practically every aspect of our lives. Gwendolyn is pretty flexible at rolling with the punches, but when she started a local public school's special education class in the fall, her teachers indicated she was not verbal. After plenty of discussions, it appeared this was how she was dealing with the trauma of a world turned upside down. She was diagnosed with selective mutism. The Portesbery School was exceptional in developing alternative means of communicating including pictures and computer programs that Gwendolyn could tap to indicate her feelings, responses, and needs. In the meantime, she remained talkative at home, though she did not often talk about her fears and anxieties. We all continued to work on creating environments conducive for the forms of communication Gwendolyn needed at the time. The staff's flexibility and tenderness helped Gwendolyn to connect with her teachers and new school surroundings and within a few months, she was talking again at school.

Shyness should not be confused with communication faults. Many people are shy, yet they may still possess or develop the skills to communicate. Many reduce their anxieties through practice and familiarity with people and environments, while others just grow out of it. Gwendolyn used to be so shy that at a summer theatre camp she declined to display her talents on the stage with her fellow campers, instead opting to march across the stage holding a poster announcing the next section of the "performance." To top it off, she hid behind the poster as she walked! Years later Gwendolyn was singing Christina Aguilera's "Beautiful" at her school's annual ball in front of 300 strangers! Strive not to let shyness get in the way of developing communication skills for your self-advocate.

At the Friends of Down Syndrome, where Gwendolyn attended a progressive day program for six years after high school, we saw many nonverbal students begin to talk and others develop advanced skills thanks to experienced teachers in a small, focused environment. Teachers and parents had to continually adjust their own communications to meet the students where they were.

Keep chipping away to best understand your self-advocate's concerns and issues. This interrogative method succeeds with patience and empathy.

Content over Style

The style of communication (pictorial, sign language, various levels of verbal) is important to recognize and is the conduit for the content of their communication. However, **we should recognize no matter the style or quantity of communication, each of our self-advocates has a lot going on in their heads.** They have the same emotions and ambitions that others do. Yet they often struggle to share those with others, even their closest friends or relatives. Imagine not being able to convey your thoughts during the day in a variety of circumstances. As an example, they are hungry for something but may not be able to share their specific interest, so they eat whatever is provided, even if it is not fulfilling. Their stomach doesn't feel well but they can't express the issue or circumstances to help decipher the specific problem and solution. Someone is bullying them at school, or a stranger approached them outside, yet they are unable to share their feelings or fears with a teacher or caregiver. They want to make their own choices but can't find the words or gestures to share their emotions and hopes. They are excited about their week ahead or scared about their ill health or a death in the family, yet they can't express these emotions. These situations may happen many times a day. We typically deal with each without much thought, yet our self-advocates are often unable to understand or share the wide range of emotions swirling around in their head.

It's no wonder depression, anxiety, and other mental health challenges are twice as prevalent in adults with developmental disabilities than the general population.[20] This is not solely a reflection of their IQ or disability itself, but largely a result of many concerns and wishes left unspoken and therefore unfulfilled. Their ability to express themselves is critical toward their independence. It is also helpful in developing our own ability to find comfort in the right level of independence for them as they move beyond the home. Thus, it is vital to help them boost their communication skills and surround them with caring support.

Rose Reif, a qualified developmental disability and mental health professional and owner of Reif Counseling Services, asserts that role modeling emotions and communication within the family is critical.[21] No topic, including death, should be off the table. While our self-advocates may be challenged to express their thoughts and emotions, they are often keen observers and eager learners. Encourage family and friends to spend time to observe, ask questions, and listen. Create more casual situations for chitchats like coffee shops or other outings. Utilize therapists, teachers, and doctors as touchpoints and contributing guides on your loved one's path to progress.

Path to Progress

Communication can be broken down between *expressive* and *receptive*. Expressive communication is more proactive, often unprompted sharing of feelings, opinions, or needs while the latter is answering specific questions. People with Down syndrome tend to be more receptive.

Our challenge is to ask broad questions and prompts instead of yes-or-no questions: "How was your math class? Tell me about your favorite hobby and show me how you do it." It's sort of a game of twenty questions. Along the way you can narrow down their thoughts and they may add some detail.

Daniel's mom, Carolyn, who we will read about in this chapter's **Family Feature**, suggests waiting at least fifteen seconds after asking a question to provide time for your self-advocate to process the question and formulate their answer. Be observant as subtle clues will help you understand more about what's going on in their head. As a result, their self-esteem is boosted through sharing while developing more expressive communication skills, whether through impromptu dialogue or using pictures or technology.

Try providing your loved one a list of topics that they may wish to share at the dinner table or other times during the day. Heather encourages her daughter Ayla to say "good morning" to other family members as part of her daily routine. Fostering and celebrating expressive dialogue reveals true personality and can be a catalyst for greater understanding amongst family members and friends.

Intense conversations are not always necessary to share care and compassion. Rose Reif also suggests getting creative. If your loved one misses a friend who has moved away or a family member who has died, try using the "empty chair exercise" to talk to someone, sharing emotions and updating them on life as if the absent person were in the room. You also might try writing great memories on the broken surfaces of a flowerpot and then gluing it back together, adding a lovely flower, and displaying it in the room as a warm gesture.[22]

Betsy Furler, trainer, speaker, author, founder and CEO of For All Abilities, insists, "They communicate with their eyes and bodies. We know they can communicate. We need them to find their words."[23]

Augmentative and alternative communication (AAC) devices can be transformative. AAC is anything used in addition to verbal speech for communication, including body language, facial expressions, and sign language. Low-tech AAC tools involve communications with pictures, photos, written messages on paper, and communication boards. Mid-tech often includes devices requiring electricity but with a lower level of customization such as a box with nine to thirty-two buttons and a simple screen. Betsy recommends high-tech devices that have dynamic displays capable of switching from one screen to another, featuring a plethora of vocabulary, along with synthesized voices. This technology is typically quite affordable, often using the self-advocate's own laptop or tablet.[24]

Frequently these high-tech devices provide great role modeling as well, as the device can talk for the self-advocate based on their screen selection of thoughts or emotions. Modeling is a great teaching tool so your loved one can make selections, hear their thoughts, and gain self-confidence. This AAC device may remain their communication companion or may be a hands-on step toward verbalization with the help of their teacher or speech therapist.[25] It may take a while for the student to gain comfort and dexterity with the device. It may be necessary to adjust the vocabulary so it is most applicable and not overwhelming. Nevertheless, Betsy encourages parents and teachers to remain diligent as high-tech AAC can be a game-changer in your self-advocate's life.[26]

Communication is essential for our self-advocate's independence—enabling them to share needs and desires, to express their thoughts and feelings, and to provide comfort and confidence. Today there are many creative approaches and assistive technologies to unlock your loved one's mind and talents.

Daniel's story is a great example of using various assistive communications to enable him to share and socialize in all settings.

Family Feature
Daniel's Story

My name is Carolyn, and I started out my career in education and have worked with people with disabilities for forty years. I had been teaching for about ten years when I moved to a small area of Florida where I met and married my husband (Gene) at the ripe old of age of thirty-seven years.

After six months into my marriage, my principal asked me if I knew anyone who be interested in adopting a child from our school. Well, God works in mysterious ways.

Daniel came to us one month shy of five years old. His fifth birthday was my first experience with trying to make social connections for him. So, I planned a party, the first of many. That first party helped connect those children to Daniel and that connection remained for many years. A birthday party tradition began. Twenty-four years later and we are still hosting a party for many, many friends that we have made along the way.

Daniel's intelligible speech was difficult at best and often nonexistent. Daniel signed when he was young and will fall back on that if he is not being understood. During his school years (and even to this day) Daniel received speech and language services to help with his communication skills. He used a variety of methods including picture symbols, voice output devices, and most recently an iPad with a communication program (Proloquo2Go).

Making friends with peers was a bit more challenging as his classmates possessed such a wide range of abilities and had some of the same communication issues. If a small group of children with the majority being "typical" were just "playing" they often left Daniel out as he could not keep up. Being left out was not on purpose or unkind. It was that he was usually just not as advanced in his play or communication skills.

As Daniel got a little older, we began involving him in outside school activities. Cub Scouts required me to assist and most often the boys and the dads were pretty helpful and nice. Occasionally one scout would befriend Daniel. Daniel loved all things scouts, including hammering, building fires, sleeping in tents, and eating hot dogs and s'mores. What more could a boy ask for?

At age of fourteen Daniel went to his first sleepover camp. It was way scarier for me than Daniel. He LOVED it and returned every summer and during many weekends camps as well. His social skills and his independence improved.

To help him prepare to transition from high school, at the age of nineteen we started a buddy club. We got together weekly with a small group of individuals with similar interests and ages. Each week a parent would take on the responsibility of planning a group activity, such as game night, scrapbooking, or dinner and a movie.

After Daniel exited school, we soon enrolled him in a local Adult Day Program by The Arc and later a faith-based half-day program where there are lots of activities and choices. Daniel attends with ten other individuals who have all become very close. They see each other as friends with something to offer and encourage each other every day.

One of the best things we have done is to get Daniel hearing aids and speech lessons. When Daniel is at his day program, he has a job to do that requires him to speak and ask questions of his peers using his voice and/or device. This has been very helpful in getting him to slow down and speak clearer.

Daniel's verbal communication has improved but he is still difficult to understand to those who don't know him. He uses a combination of verbal communication, signs, and prompts with his iPad.

Daniel has discovered the value of his iPad in various situations. He can order a cheeseburger and everything he wants on it with no help—it is very motivating. If the person sees it as their voice and sees its power, they will use it independently.

If I was going to give advice to a family I would suggest starting early, trying everything, and working hard to develop and maintain friendships. If you look around and don't find what is best for your loved one, make it happen. Most likely there are other parents or families looking for something just like you!

Fast forward twenty-four years and my son Daniel has now turned twenty-nine. It has been a wonderful ride with a lot of curves and ups and downs. He has enriched our lives and made me a better teacher and way better person.

Carolyn, Daniel's mom

Chapter 6
Safety & Security

Safety and security understandably arise as the primary concerns for parents and caregivers when it comes to adult independence.[27] Parents worry about all their children and family members, but this especially applies to those who appear more vulnerable. Most people with Down syndrome assume the best in people. Concepts and terms such as "devious" and "evil" don't really compute for them. Even when someone at school appears to be mean, that confuses them because they assume the best in others. Thus, our forewarning to be cautious seems foreign to them.

However, the Autism Housing Network notes over 60 percent of individuals with intellectual/developmental disabilities are victims of abuse. "Abuse is prevalent." Twenty-five percent of persons with autism are sexually abused and 44 percent have been abused more than ten times. These are astounding and frightening numbers.[28] Similar statistics likely apply to the Down syndrome community. Yet, we can't shield our loved ones by just keeping them at home. We must equip them with the skills and safeguards to support themselves and their independence. Until safety and security are aptly addressed, the thought of our self-advocate operating on their own, whether at work, commuting, or living in their own home, can be rattling.

While this risk will never fully disappear for any of our children, we can take steps to put protections in place.

Engaging with Strangers

In chapter 4 we discussed the Social Circles Model, a process for categorizing engagements and better understanding appropriate and inappropriate contact. Although dangers and abuse do exist within the more familiar groups, typically the greatest risk lies in the "strangers" category. A robust teaching approach includes discussing and role-playing various scenarios:

A clerk at a store says hello: It is appropriate to return the gesture but not to provide personal details like phone number or home address unless required for a transaction.

A person approaches you while you are grocery shopping alone: You may wish to say hello but keep a watchful eye and decline any assistance or conversation. These are difficult situations because most people are just friendly and want to be helpful, but if your self-advocate has a hard time distinguishing intent or in defending themselves if the encounter goes awry, best to avoid such engagements in the first place.

Another student bullies you at school: Leave the situation and find safety with friends and teachers. Report the situation to the teacher and avoid that person when possible. Everyone deserves to learn, work, and live without bullying.

A stranger invites you to walk with them or get in their car: This is a clear "no." The catch is that strangers and criminals are professional and quite devious. They may say the parents asked to pick them up or they may lure them with candy. When this scenario was presented to dozens of adults with Down syndrome at the Friends of Down Syndrome in Houston, 85 percent said getting in that car would be okay![29]

The first step to manage these risks is openly discussing them. You don't want to overwhelm or scare your self-advocate, so you may offer this conversation in small doses, but you must have the discussion. Talk through the scenarios and nuances like candy and trickery. Ask what they think and what they would do. Role play these scenarios when you are out and consider testing your loved one as well. Ask a friend of yours who your self-advocate doesn't know to engage with your loved one in nonphysical conversation when you are not standing nearby. You may observe or get a report-out from your friend and then have discussions with your loved one afterwards. As Daniel's mom, Carolyn, recognizes, **"We can teach stranger danger all day long, but we will not ever know unless we test them to see if they apply what they have learned."**

Train your self-advocate to become more aware of their surroundings—the people around them and signage for exits or assistance. Joyce asks Amanda to remember where they park and guide them back to the car later, noticing certain things about buildings along the way in order to raise Amanda's level of awareness.

These approaches will help self-advocates understand appropriate behavior and manage their own actions accordingly. But we must also have a conversation when someone else violates the appropriateness of a relationship. This could be a friend bullying or pushing them at school, a close family member or friend trying to touch them inappropriately, or a stranger trying to strike up a conversation or lure them into a car. Many abuses go unknown. Watch for uncommon behaviors or reclusiveness and encourage your self-advocate to share those situations with you or an authority figure in a safe place. Otherwise, when left to their own devices, they may feel unwarranted shame or guilt and not learn how to prevent such situations in the future.

As you practice each of these scenarios, your loved one will become more confident in their actions, and you will become more comfortable in their abilities. Still, you will need to assess the comfort level of yourself and your self-advocate in remaining safe and secure in various situations. Maybe together you choose certain work opportunities based on the engagement frequency with strangers and the level of oversight offered. Perhaps some independent living options lack provisions to meet your security requirements and are therefore struck off the list. Marbridge Foundation, a nationally renowned residential living community in Texas, shares their approach to safety and security in this chapter's **Expert Advice**.

It is impossible to remove all safety and security risks for your self-advocate, or for any of your kids or even yourself. However, discussions and practice can mitigate the risks to an acceptable level. **Merely keeping your self-advocate at home, away from others is never the best solution.** We must make safety and security a priority in your Independence Plan so your self-advocate can be safe while still enjoying the opportunities to work, live, and love.

Around the Home

Home should be a comforting place for everyone, filled with loved ones, support, hobbies, and warmth. However, it also includes personal risks worth identifying and mitigating. Your self-advocate should be aware of the hazards around the house, especially in the kitchen. Whether you are ready for them to operate appliances like the dishwasher, garbage disposal, microwave, stovetop, oven, or knives on the countertop, they still need to understand the risks. How many of us have flipped the wrong switch and suddenly the garbage disposal starts whirring? Who would know that tin foil and forks don't belong in the microwave unless they are told or experience the sparks? We've probably all leaned against stovetop buttons before. All these hazards should be reviewed and explained. Until you are comfortable your loved one clearly understands the risks and how to stay away or operate each, keep safeguards (stovetop button covers or microwave door locks, for example) in place.

Other hazards scattered around the house include electric sockets and light plugs, the risk of small appliances near bathtubs or sinks, ceiling fans above beds that act as trampolines, and front and back doors that provide escape routes for wanderers and entry points for strangers. Security systems to ensure doors are locked and water isn't overflowing from the bathtub are available. The security and peace of mind may be well worth the investment.

Home Alone

Leaving your self-advocate home alone is both empowering for them and life-changing for you. The self-advocate achieves a significant level of independence—a stair-step change that may seem overwhelming to them but most often feels overdue. For the parent, this step suddenly breaks that bond of 100 percent codependency and begins to suggest further independence is possible for the self-advocate and family alike.

As with all our kids, there is no specific age that works for all self-advocates. You need to assess their preparedness while readying your mindset as well.

This is clearly not a simple step but requires preparation and practice. In advance, discuss together what being home alone would mean and when you both believe the time is right. Explain that the challenge is not in the routine but the exception. The vast majority of the time, everything will go smoothly during their time alone. However, exceptions are what everyone must be prepared for. What to do if someone calls (for those with landlines)? What if someone knocks on the door? What if they say they are the police? What if a smoke alarm or security alarm goes off? What if he/she doesn't feel well? What if a fire breaks out in the house? All these scenarios are unlikely, yet plausible. Our guidance with Gwendolyn was that she should call us under all these circumstances but if she can't contact us, she should dial 9-1-1 and state her name, address, and issue. If there is a fire, she should exit the house immediately and go to a neighbor's house and call us and 9-1-1. It's important to rehearse these scenarios together and later include unannounced drills.

When you are ready to go to the next level, first practice by pretending to be out of the house while staying in your room. Next you can rehearse by being in the car outside, at a neighbor's house, or a nearby restaurant. Be sure your cell phone (and that of your self-advocate) are charged and not on mute in case you get a call. Don't be surprised to get some calls. It can take some time to build comfort and confidence. Having a home alarm system and a video doorbell will help give you peace of mind since you can become aware of any issue, even if your self-advocate doesn't remember to call you immediately.

Leave a "cheat sheet" for your self-advocate next to the front door and in the kitchen that they can reference rather than panic. Include your phone number, 9-1-1, and the info they should share if they must call 9-1-1. After several practices, they will begin to master this important step and you will begin to see new possibilities.

Modern Technology

It is helpful for our self-advocates to have their own smart phones and social media accounts, but as with all users, restraint is necessary. Gwendolyn has had her own cell phone since she became a teenager. We can call and text each other at any time. We also use the "Find My Friend" app to know her location while she is commuting, at school, or at work. Naturally, this convenience can be abused. Our daughter has gotten quite adept at surfing the web. She once used the internet to monitor her classmates' fundraising efforts for her school's annual ball. She so wanted her best friend to win that she submitted her own online pledge of nearly $10,000 herself! Thankfully, school administrators called us to see if this was truly our intent. The "donation" was removed, and we had a long discussion about the proper use of the internet, money, and responsibility. A friend shared a story of their son with Down syndrome arranging his own moving van online to expedite his dream of moving out. Don't underestimate their abilities.

Obviously, there are also dangerous elements in social media and the internet. It seems like daily we receive spam and luring advertisements, not to mention inappropriate invitations or images. It is certainly prudent to have conversations about these elements before providing a phone, laptop, or tablet. I would also advocate periodically checking their email received and sent and website history to ensure your self-advocate remains safe and protected.

It is, honestly, impossible for parents to keep anyone completely safe. With a strong dose of forewarning, training, and precautions, we allow measured risks for our children because, while we want to protect them, we also recognize they need to be equipped to thrive in the world. This includes being aware of and managing the negative elements. Rather than limiting our self-advocates' access, we need to prepare and practice with them, to minimize risks while preserving opportunities.

Becca McPherson is the vice president of development at Marbridge Foundation. They are reminded of the challenges and concerns around safety and security every time they meet and tour a new family and take their responsibility quite seriously. In our **Expert Advice** for this chapter, Becca shares the steps Marbridge takes to ensure safety and security. You may consider these practices when evaluating day programs and living communities for your loved one.

Expert Advice
Marbridge Story

For as long as time, the running joke with parents is that children aren't born with a handbook. But parents continually work hard at navigating the good, the bad, and the hard, with the end goal to raise a child that is safe and can thrive within their own abilities. That will obviously look different for every child, but the consistent goal is safety, happiness, and well-being.

With a child born with any type of disability, families tackle these goals in different ways and there are quite a few resources available. For many families, finding, utilizing, and navigating these resources can be a full-time job, and in most cases, on top of already having a full-time career to be able to afford access. In today's world, family members who have navigated the sometimes muddy and murky waters of finding services, programs, and resources can share the struggles and success they went through in hopes of laying a better path to help other families.

The Marbridge Mission

Marbridge is one of those resources. Established in 1953, Ed and Marge Bridges set out with a goal to find a program for their son Jim who was born with intellectual and developmental disabilities (I/DD). As their search stretched through the 1940s, they didn't feel comfortable with the options available at the time and set out to write a new chapter in the history of serving those with I/DD. This new chapter consisted of obtaining hundreds of acres just south of Austin, Texas, dedicated to helping those with disabilities learn the skills and trades to contribute to the greater community in amazing ways.

The Bridges designed their programs to serve the needs of the individuals living at Marbridge and not to force them to learn skills they may not have inherently possessed. Jobs were designed for the abilities the residents had and felt confident in doing. Throughout the years, the Bridges watched the struggles Jim had as he aged and continued expanding the campus to provide not only for Jim's needs, but the needs of so many other individuals who had I/DD. By the 1980s, Marbridge had established a semi-independent living community, an assisted living community, and perhaps the first licensed skilled nursing facility in the nation to specifically serve adults with cognitive and intellectual disabilities.

Marbridge now serves 275 adults with I/DD through the established three care communities, offering residents up to 150 training and education opportunities through a trimester system.

Safety at the Forefront

As the greater community began growing and engaging more with Marbridge residents and their talents, it became clear through the years that Marbridge residents were mastering jobs and independent living skills to also give back to the greater community. More residents were learning to ride public transportation and engage the public through jobs at local grocery stores, airports, hospitals, and more. Marbridge celebrated these accomplishments but also knew these types of opportunities opened individuals up to the harshness of the "real world."

According to *Disability Justice,* "[a]buse and exploitation are constant dangers for people with developmental disabilities.[30] In fact, they are four to ten times more likely to be abused than their peers without disabilities. Compared to the general population, people with developmental disabilities are at greatest risk of abuse," neglect, and exploitation. This is one of the reasons that residential campuses like Marbridge, who offer abilities-centered training, caregiver support, and the opportunity to live in a safe environment from young adulthood through end of life, are vital to the success of many adults with I/DD.

So, what does safety look like for the aforementioned adult with Down syndrome or anybody with I/DD? This can take many forms. In 2018, the Administration for Community Living (ACL) published an article talking about "Seeing Me for Me"[31] and identifying that people with disabilities want the greater community "to look beyond someone's disability and see each individual as a whole person. They want to live in the community, work and earn a living wage, go to school or college, have friends, go on dates, lead a healthy life, and be active in a faith or other social community." This is exactly the goal that Marbridge strives to make happen every day.

Prioritizing Safety

Marbridge has built a community where individuals learn daily living tasks, participate in training and educational classes that can last a lifetime, and learn independent living and job skills, while maintaining their own space and living their best lives with friends. Helping these residents thrive as independently as possible in their homes takes planning at an extraordinary level, with safety being at the top. Prioritizing safety in the twenty-first century versus 1953 looks vastly different.

A campus as large as Marbridge must have every "player" in a resident's life working together. This requires families, direct care employees, dietitians and nutritionists, therapists and counselors, physicians and medical personnel, educators, boards, licensing, and most importantly, the resident to have input into providing a safe environment to thrive. In today's world, many residents come with digital communication devices, whether that be phones or speech devices. Digital safety and security are now just as important as physical safety.

Visual cues are set up throughout campus for residents who can and cannot read, along with braille for those with visual impairments, so residents can easily and independently navigate campus. Residents are accounted for frequently throughout the day and are visually observed during the night. Cameras set up in main living areas and throughout campus, including at exits, can help to visually see residents without infringing on their everyday lives, while still ensuring they are safe and active. Electronic devices and social accounts are encouraged but monitored closely to ensure that relationships are healthy and productive. Families and Marbridge staff communicate frequently about loved ones to try and anticipate health issues or any risks before they become a problem or an issue.

In addition, an "Emergency Management Plan" is reviewed at least annually addressing issues such as an active shooter, wildfire, and infectious disease, and designates which resources and personnel should be contacted. In any situation, communication is paramount:

- Phone systems are through web access and have an "all page" capacity.

- Messenger service notifies all staff, residents, and families in an emergency situation.
- Strong Wi-Fi throughout campus ensures that communication will rarely, if ever, be down.
- All three care communities have two-way radios and cell phones for on-call supervisors and persons in remote portions of the campus or in vehicles.
- Each part of campus has 24/7 awake staff.

Additionally, there are at least annual campus reviews by the local fire marshal and fire chief, state licensing representative, Texas Commission on Environmental Quality, and more.

In today's ever-changing world, it will always feel impossible to keep up with everything, which is the reason Marbridge has developed a wholistic approach to serving adults with I/DD. This method includes everyone who is active in a resident's life to provide an environment in which every person has the opportunity to thrive through safety, well-being, and happiness, while living *a whole new life.*

Becca McPherson, Marbridge VP of Development

SECTION III
FOUNDATIONS FOR THE FUTURE

This section is packed with information essential to fulfilling your responsibility as the parent, caregiver, or guardian of your loved one. Your eyes need to be wide open to both the medical and financial challenges as your self-advocate grows toward adult independence. As people with Down syndrome are living longer, more are outliving their parents. Thus, managing health issues and extended financial requirements are growing challenges for our community.

This section lays out common health risks and how to foster good habits. It also describes the complex world of public resources and how to navigate the rules to ensure your family receives, maintains, and protects the maximum proceeds possible to support the long independence journey ahead. We will also cover legal vehicles such as guardianship, ABLE accounts, and special needs trusts so you have the full range of tools at your disposal.

Section III: Plans and Actions		
#	Action	Life Stage*
1	Select & educate your medical team	Early Childhood
2	Screen for common health risks	Childhood
3	Print, review, share the Global Down Syndrome Medical Care Guidelines	Adolescence

#	Action	Life Stage*
4	NTG: EDSD Alzheimer's screening	Adulthood
5	Update your downloadable Independence Plan with critical timelines and actions	Adolescence
6	Create a rough lifetime budget	Adolescence
7	Apply for SSI services (waiver programs)	After Birth
8	Apply for SSI benefits	Age 18
9	Learn about earnings & asset limitations to maintain SSI eligibility	Before Employment
10	Learn about links to parent's RSDI benefits and how to preserve eligibility	Before Employment
11	Apply for age waiver to remain on parent's private medical insurance	Age 26
12	Apply for parent's RSDI upon their disability, retirement, and/or death	Parental Event
13	Consider guardianship	Age 18
14	Setup ABLE account	Before Employment
15	Create and update last will and testament	Early Childhood, Adolescence, Adulthood
16	Create special needs trust(s)	Early Childhood
17	Apply for HIPP, if applicable	Age 18
18	Apply for SNAP benefits	Age 18
19	Create and update letter of intent	Early Childhood, Adolescence, Adulthood
20	Create and update documentation filing system	Early Childhood, Adolescence, Adulthood

If your loved one has passed this stage but has not completed this action, place this at the top of your action plan

Check out resources and references at the back of the book. Downloads are available for free at:

http://www.beyonddownsyndrome.net/The-Essential-Guide

Chapter 7
Health & Wellness

Though many parents have tended to numerous health challenges for their loved one since birth, it is especially important to be aware of those common health risks for adults with Down syndrome as well. Caregivers of loved ones at any age should be aware of the risks and steps to manage these conditions now.

According to Tara Goodwin, D.O. of the Adult Down Syndrome Clinic of Questcare Dallas[32] who specializes in health care for people with Down syndrome, "the twenty-first chromosome is not a 'bad' chromosome. The health-related issues we see as more prevalent [in people with Down syndrome] are most likely due to the trisomy... the **excess** of particular genes that may be overexpressed."[33] Nevertheless, **this longer life span means families are grappling with health conditions for longer periods, as well as confronting new issues as people age into their fifties and sixties.** Parents and caregivers play indispensable roles in ensuring recent and future advances benefit our loved ones.

To build your own knowledge and equip yourself to advocate with the medical team, start with this chapter. Learn more through the Global Down Syndrome's Medical Care Guidelines for Adults with Down Syndrome publication found in the resources section of this book. Share both with your loved one's medical team. Make sure they are prepared to learn and engage on these topics with your family. Use medical appointments as opportunities for your self-advocate to learn about their bodies and how to talk about their physical and emotional feelings. Empower them to take steps to take care of themselves.

Six Most Common Health Risks for Adults with Down Syndrome

Six common health issues plague most people with Down syndrome throughout their adult lives. The prevalence of these conditions within our community may surprise you and your medical team. If your loved one has been diagnosed with any of these, pay attention to the management tips listed. Otherwise, have your medical team screen for each of these at appropriate intervals. Dr. Tara Goodwin has contributed to the information below and supports the need for families to educate themselves.

1. **Hypothyroidism**: Your brain's hypothalamus produces a hormone that tells the pituitary gland to make a thyroid-stimulating hormone (TSH). If your body has an underactive thyroid or doesn't produce enough hormones, hypothyroidism results.
   a. Prevalence: 5 to 10 percent of the general public,[34] approximately 40 to 50 percent of people with Down syndrome[35]
   b. Onset: In Down syndrome, this is most commonly related to congenital hypothyroidism, which is usually identified at birth, or to an autoimmune disorder called Hashimoto's thyroiditis that can develop later in life.
   c. Symptoms: Thyroid hormones are important to every cell in the body, and therefore hypothyroidism can

cause a multitude of symptoms including low energy, muscle pain or weakness, difficulty thinking and focusing, behavioral changes and irritability, weight gain, impaired cognition, constipation, lethargy, dry skin, slowed speech, and more.

d. Prevention: There are no particular preventative steps. Because many symptoms of hypothyroidism are common in individuals with Down syndrome who *do not* have hypothyroidism, it is important to screen regularly. Pediatric guidelines recommend newborn screening and again at six months, followed by annual screening thereafter.

e. Management: Frequent monitoring of levels may be needed while taking thyroid replacement medication in order to ensure the correct dosing.

f. Repercussions: If unchecked, hypothyroidism can result in less energy and lower metabolism (hence weight gain) as well as slower cognitive development, all of which are already challenges for adults with Down syndrome.

2. **Obstructive Sleep Apnea (OSA)**: Due to anatomic abnormalities more common in Down syndrome like narrower passageways and other comorbidities like hypotonia and obesity, sleep apnea is quite common in the Down syndrome community.

a. Prevalence: 26 percent of the general public ages thirty to seventy,[36] approximately 60 percent of children with Down syndrome by age four.[37]

b. Onset: Often starts as a baby/toddler and can increase in severity as one ages.

c. Symptoms: 53 percent of individuals diagnosed with OSA have no associated symptoms like snoring[38] but still can suffer from cessation of breathing during sleep, daytime drowsiness or irritability, mouth breathing or nasal voice, and restlessness during sleep.

d. Prevention: There are no particular steps to prevent sleep apnea. Pediatric guidelines recommend a sleep study at age three to five years.

e. Management: See your doctor at the earliest sign for testing. Sometimes tonsils or adenoids will be removed to improve breathing. Adjunctive therapies like nasal steroids, palatal expansion, uvulectomy, or oropharyngeal (back of the throat) exercises can also be helpful. Often the doctor will eventually prescribe a continuous positive pressure ventilation device (CPAP) to be worn during sleep. With support and practice, this can become part of your child's nighttime routine. Multiple research studies on hypoglossal nerve stimulators are currently underway involving children and adults with Down syndrome. These implanted stimulators have been shown to improve obstruction in the general population.

f. Repercussions: If unchecked, OSA can result in poor sleep and low energy, but also hypertension, heart issues, behavioral issues, decreased cognitive abilities, and/or reduced growth rate.

3. **Obesity**: Many adolescents and adults with Down syndrome are overweight and obese due to slower metabolism, often

exacerbated by hypothyroidism, obstructive sleep apnea, stubbornness, or a lack of inclusion in group activities.

a. Prevalence: 16 to 18 percent of general public adolescents,[39] approximately 30-50 percent of children with Down syndrome.[40]

b. Onset: Often starts as a toddler and increases in severity during adolescence.

c. Symptoms: Includes interest to eat on a schedule and when others eat, without recognition of when they are truly hungry. Low metabolism and lack of exercise contributes to weight gain, even when overeating is not obvious.

d. Prevention: Introduce nutritional training, hunger awareness, and exercise from the earliest age to become part of their lifelong routine.

e. Management: Doctors and nutritionists can provide some guidance. Talking about nutrition, food groups, and hunger awareness around the dinner table can be quite helpful. Starting at age twenty-one, adults with Down syndrome should be screened for type 2 diabetes every two to three years.[41]

f. Repercussions: If unchecked, can result in skin infections, lung and heart disease, as well as cancer or arthritis. Obesity can complicate obstructive sleep apnea and mental health as well.

4. **Celiac Disease**: While celiac disease is not overly common in people with Down syndrome, the community is six times more likely to contract this disease than the general population.[42]

a. Prevalence: 1 to 3 percent of the typical populations and approximately 5 to 20 percent of individuals with Down syndrome will have celiac disease.

b. Onset: It can occur across the lifespan.

c. Symptoms: Includes poor weight gain, diarrhea, vomiting, constipation, anemia, nutritional deficiencies, irritability, and behavior changes.

d. Prevention: Because symptoms can overlap with some traits common to Down syndrome, it is important to screen. There are no pediatric guidelines addressing testing, but adult practice guidelines recommend annual screening for symptoms and appropriate testing if there is concern. Testing includes a screening blood test and possibly a small bowel biopsy to confirm.

e. Management: Treatment involves following a gluten-free regimen that eliminates all wheat, barley, and rye from the diet as well as cross-contamination with these foods.

f. Repercussions: Delayed diagnosis can lead to malnutrition, decreased growth, neuropathies, osteoporosis, and certain intestinal lymphomas.

5. **Mental Health**: Well beyond the intellectual/developmental disability diagnosis, lack of inclusion at school, at home, or in their own future plans impacts their mental condition. Additionally, obesity and poor communication skills affect their ability to share their emotional state and concerns, often resulting in mental health issues by adulthood. Since the prevalence of mental health concerns has more to do with the environment and support than genetics, the frequency of

these issues within the Down syndrome community could revert toward the general population more so than the other common health issues noted.

a. Prevalence: Mental health issues such as anxiety, obsessive-compulsive disorder (OCD), and depression are twice as likely in individuals with Down syndrome.[43] While this could be understated as the diagnosis itself can be difficult to attain for those with cognitive disabilities, it is also common for normal characteristics of people within the I/DD community to be misread as mental health issues.

b. Onset: Often starts in adolescence and can increase in severity as one ages.

c. Symptoms: Inattentiveness, new behavioral issues, sluggishness, skills regression, and new fears of familiar objects or routine events can be signs of mental health issues. On the other hand, characteristics that are common in people with Down syndrome should not be misconstrued as mental illness, including self-talk, delayed or absent verbal skills, "grooves" or routines, repetition and lack of flexibility, tendency toward concrete thinking and difficulty with abstract ideas, distorted time concept, slower processing speeds, poor expressive communication skills with strong receptive skills. Parents, teachers, and caregivers should not be too quick to just mark this up to their Down syndrome or I/DD diagnosis but should delve further seeking to understand root causes. *The Diagnostic and Statistical Manual of Mental Disorders* and the *Diagnostic*

Manual-Intellectual Disability 2 may also be used to assist with diagnosis.[44]

d. Prevention: Mental health issues may not always be preventable but especially for people with Down syndrome, helping them understand their emotions and discussing their concerns may help address issues early.

e. Management: Consider specially trained therapists as an ongoing resource to help people with Down syndrome to recognize issues, share them, and find implementable solutions. Event-specific issues surrounding family illnesses, death, relocation, or change of routine (including most recently the COVID-19 pandemic) can prompt traumatic responses.[45] Anticipate these events and ensure a support system of family, close friends, and therapists is prepared to assist. Adults with Down syndrome may also bundle similar memories or emotional events together so triggering one may introduce recall of a series of events that can become overwhelming. Unbundling such events and encouraging appropriate responses to issues (e.g., a construed nudge or insult by a classmate does not warrant the same response as recollecting the death of a family member) can help develop stronger coping skills.

f. Repercussions: If unchecked, mental health issues can result in skills regression (deterioration of their educational, vocational, and/or social skills), overeating, decreased self-esteem and confidence, and perhaps the earlier onset of dementia.

6. Alzheimer's Disease: Recent research indicates that one of the genes responsible for Alzheimer's disease, the "Alzheimer's gene," resides on the twenty-first chromosome. **Due to the overexpression of this chromosome related to trisomy, the frequency, speed, and severity of Alzheimer's disease among the Down syndrome population is notably higher than the general population.** It is hypothesized that one reason for faster progression of Alzheimer's in any population is related to lower baseline cognition.[46]

a. Prevalence: 16 percent of adults in the general population,[47] **75 percent** of adults with Down syndrome during their lifetime,[48] and notably 50 percent by age sixty, 30 percent by age fifty.[49]

b. Onset: Signs of Alzheimer's can set in as early as their thirties. By age forty, almost all brains of people with Down syndrome have proteins that are Alzheimer's markers. Research shows that changes in the brain occur, but symptoms do not tend to develop for another five to ten years.[50] Alzheimer's should be a diagnosis of exclusion. It is important to rule out other causes of symptoms before making the diagnosis, especially in individuals younger than forty.

c. Symptoms: Most are similar to the general population including forgetfulness, lack of motivation, belligerence, and new discomfort with old routines. However, one exception is that seizures are more common, effecting 77 percent in those with Down syndrome compared with 2 to 25 percent in the general population, resulting in swallowing difficulty, gait disturbances, and change in personality or behavior, all of which can hasten death.[51]

d. Prevention: There is no particular prevention, but cognitive disabilities can accelerate the disease, so greater cognitive engagement (learning through education, work, and exposure to new experiences) may help delay the onset. Some indications are that Alzheimer's occurs most often with learning challenges, hypertension, obesity, diabetes, low physical activity, obstructive sleep apnea, and low social contact, all of which are prevalent with Down syndrome.

e. Management: Alzheimer's disease tends to progress much faster in adults with Down syndrome, often leading to death just three to six years after diagnosis. Pay attention to the symptoms and seek to address the preventative conditions noted above. The National Task Group provides considerable information including a test, Early Detection and Screening for Dementia, NTG-EDSD, that can be taken annually to gauge "(1) cognition, memory, and executive function, (2) behavior and personality, (3) communication, (4) adaptive functioning, (5) ambulatory and motor skills, and (6) general decline in established skills."[52] Consider how your loved one may be attended to if/when Alzheimer's sets in. Some living communities provide sustainable memory care services. There are no medical treatments approved for use in those with Down syndrome and Alzheimer's at this time. Treatment for symptoms like depression, insomnia, and agitation may be helpful. Nonmedical treatments may have the most impact on day-to-day function, including using visuals, being aware of sensory processing, and using adaptive tools in accommodating one's environment.

f. Repercussions: There is currently no prevention or cure for Alzheimer's disease. However, there is a lot of research working toward a cure, much of which overlaps Down syndrome given the shared twenty-first chromosome.

Dual Diagnosis: Down Syndrome and Autism Spectrum Disorder (ASD)

Many parents who are navigating their child's development with Down syndrome discover later that their loved one also has autism. Dual diagnosis of Down syndrome and autism is not uncommon (12 to 41 percent of people with Down syndrome)[53] but it is often misdiagnosed or identified much later in life.

Dr. Sari Bar, medical director of the Down Syndrome Clinic at Children's Health Dallas campus, attributes much of this problem as "overshadowing," when a health professional assumes the child's cognitive or behavior challenges are part of their disability of Down syndrome and fail to explore further.[54] While it is proper that families and doctors first rule out the common health conditions affecting people with Down syndrome, often doctors misconstrue warning signs of autism as symptoms of Down syndrome.

Early diagnosis of autism is quite important in preparing a course of action. According to Dr. Bar, "In general, compared to people with Down syndrome without autism, it is more common for people with dual diagnosis to have:

- Difficulties with communication, social engagement, sensory sensitivities, and behavioral challenges

- Restricted or repetitive behaviors
- Significant cognitive challenges, resulting in slower processing speeds"[55]

Dr. Bar advises that parents consult with an expert in dual diagnosis who may run tests and observations to determine conclusions. The challenges of dual diagnosis are explored further through Chaya's and Ethan's stories, featured at the end of this chapter and chapter 11, respectively.

Other Medical Conditions

Certainly, there are other health risks for adults with Down syndrome, many of which are common at birth such as gastrointestinal complications, cervical (atlantoaxial) instability issues, and congenital heart disease (CHD), the latter of which affects 50 percent of the Down syndrome community. Each should be addressed quite early and monitored throughout their lives. Vision and hearing loss are quite common and are typically addressed with glasses and hearing aids if necessary. With the aging population, arthritis and osteoporosis could become more common within the Down syndrome population as well.

According to Dr. Bar, "children with Down syndrome are at higher risk of having specific vitamin or nutrient deficiencies due to poor diet or low intake. Low iron is of specific concern because it is a vital nutrient for early childhood brain development."[56] Iron levels should be monitored and supplemented as needed.

It is rare for individuals with Down syndrome to develop solid tumors in the same prevalence we see in the general population. For instance, while lung, colon, breast, and prostate cancers remain the most common cancers in the general population, individuals with Down syndrome are less likely to develop these tumors. However, people with Down syndrome are more likely at risk for leukemia/lymphoma, melanoma, and testicular cancer and should be screened for these accordingly. In addition, though congenital heart disease is more prevalent in Down syndrome, predisposition to heart attacks or strokes is less common.[57]

General Health Approach

The *Alzheimer's Disease & Down Syndrome Guidebook* includes these four tips for adults with Down syndrome to stay healthy:[58]

1. Participate in regular cardiovascular exercise like walking or biking.
2. Eat a healthy and balanced diet.
3. Stay mentally stimulated and engaged.
4. Stay socially engaged.

We'll cover the first two in this health chapter and the latter two in section IV, Taking on the World. Suffice to say, your self-advocate's general health condition, as well as management of the common health issues above, benefits greatly from a focus on nutrition, fitness, and medication. Forming and reinforcing these healthy habits is a lifelong priority. First, a word about metabolism, since it spans all three of these general health approaches.

Boosting Metabolism

Metabolism is often lower in the Down syndrome community than the general population. As with society overall, metabolism does steadily slow with age, typically from about forty. Thus, the opportunity to spark your loved one's metabolism is early.

WebMD shares various methods that may contribute to improved metabolism:

- Strength training and high intensity aerobic exercises
- Smaller, more frequent meals and healthy snacks
- Replacing carbohydrates with proteins
- Drinking water along with modest amounts of coffee or green tea[59]

Perhaps the most important catalyst for improved metabolism is maintaining proper thyroid levels as discussed in the previous section.

Nutrition

Let's face it—this can be a difficult subject for most adults. Our kids may be further challenged with slow metabolism and a lack of fat-burning physical fitness options. Thus, we should strive to get ahead of this issue and instill positive nutritional habits at a young age. We don't suddenly crave fruits and vegetables or cut our portion sizes in half after learning to stack carbs on our plates for over a decade. Introducing and role modeling these positive routines with all your kids will reinforce healthy habits.

This is one area we continue to struggle with for Gwendolyn, so I completely get it. Life is busy and parenting can be an overwhelming learning process. We all do our best and must take pride in our successes and not lament our shortcomings. But as I reflect, this is one area that Gwendolyn certainly would have benefited from greater guidance at an earlier stage. I know this is hard for many, but our loved ones learn so much from observing what we do.

That said, Gwendolyn has taken several nutrition classes that have helped her understand the value of certain foods and the risks of others. She can recite them ad nauseum. However, her biggest challenge, like mine and many others, is the willpower to say "no" as well as recognizing when she is truly hungry. Offering a wide variety of foods promotes exploration and balanced nourishment. This is best taught by modeling and discussion while shopping in the grocery store, cooking in the kitchen, and sharing a meal around the dinner table. We all benefit from this approach more than the adage many of us grew up with, "think of the poor, starving children in _____ and finish your plate." If you remember that, it's a testament to the impact of statements from early childhood and the opportunity to instill more positive mantras from an early age.

Good nutritional habits help manage several of the top six risks including obesity, obstructive sleep apnea, and celiac disease. A healthy body is a source of pride and self-confidence, yet it is also important not to body-shame those that struggle in this area. Such mistreatment rarely changes one's trajectory and can have a catastrophic impact to self-esteem and mental health.

Supportive habits reach beyond what is on the plate and how much is eaten. Snacking out of boredom, offering foods as a behavioral incentive, or eating in front of the TV all send a negative message to our self-advocates. Instilling good nutritional habits should be purposeful. Consider using checklists or visual aids such as the nutritional plates that depict proper food group representation and portion size to take advantage of your self-advocate's visual learning methods.

Proper hydration is another often overlooked aspect of nutrition. The Mayo Clinic suggest drinking sixty-four to 100 ounces of water a day[60] through a variety of forms including water, other non-sugar drinks, and various fruits and vegetables. (Watermelon and spinach are nearly 100 percent water weight.) You can count the ounces to ensure proper hydration, but the most revealing sign is clear to light yellow urine.

This has always been an issue for Gwendolyn. She eats her meals sequentially and water is never part of any stage of her plan. We are still encouraging her to drink during each stage and throughout the day, but I'm sure she remains deficient. This can be a much bigger issue in hot climates. We're also discovering that a lack of water means her veins are less than prominent, so drawing blood from Gwendolyn is always a challenge, usually requiring a few jabs in arms and hands. As with other nutritional issues, instilling a habit of drinking water benefits from modeling and early childhood introduction.

Fitness and Exercise

While most adolescents and adults with Down syndrome suffer from being overweight or obese, it doesn't have to be that way. There are many fit self-advocates who tend to follow the steps shared here. Incorporate exercise into their day by incorporating it into your day and bringing them along. If you run or bike or play soccer, include them. They will recognize this is a normal part of the day and they will want to be included. It really doesn't have to be exhaustive. Just moving around, stretching, and taking walks makes a huge difference. For those with limited mobility, work with occupational and physical therapy to create an appropriate movement program.

Unfortunately, our family is a testament to the difficulties many families face. I only began an exercise routine myself when Gwendolyn was about ten. Up to that point, her stubbornness and my impatience meant I picked her up and put her on my shoulders when she was tired of walking and just plopped herself on the ground. This started quite early but became a game that extended until she was around ten…and much too heavy for my back to reasonably support her ride. I'm sure I've lost a few inches in height due to compacted vertebrae. Don't let this happen to you. Not only did I suffer, but Gwendolyn's metabolism was sacrificed and more importantly, we missed an opportunity to support her own independence. Gwendolyn walks on her own now but has never embraced much exercise until recently.

She enjoys Special Olympics basketball and bocce, and she now rides her trike around campus most days. She walks to her classes throughout the week and has several cardio and exercise classes as well. However, her low metabolism appears "immovable" and has made any weight loss appear nearly impossible, despite her much more active lifestyle and structured menu since moving to her new home in her mid-twenties. This is another example of the power of early intervention.

Medications and Devices

Gwendolyn now takes a variety of pills and uses a CPAP machine at night. We have been diligent in having doctors involve her in medical appointments and diagnoses. We explain why certain pills may be prescribed and the importance of taking her pills as instructed. She is familiar with what each pill looks like and can typically spot if she is missing one. Gwendolyn sometimes gets distracted and occasionally forgets to take her pills. Setting an alarm on a smart phone helps her stay on schedule. At her residential living community, the staff administer her pills, but she keeps a close eye out as well.

Gwendolyn has used a CPAP machine for years to address her sleep apnea. She quickly learned how to put the mask on and immediately adopted the habit. She is sure to bring her CPAP with her on home visits or vacation trips. She is less diligent in using a cleaning machine and needs others to order and change masks and tubes as recommended. Again, the staff at her living community takes care of that but we do check for tank cleanliness and any rash around her mask when we see her on FaceTime or on our personal visits.

Connecting your self-advocate with their medical conditions and prescriptions is quite important in empowering them in their person-centered plan. As the Six Most Common Health Risks section notes, many conditions afflict adolescents and adults with Down syndrome, all of which necessitate awareness and management by self-advocates and their families.

Medical Engagement

Regardless of whether your loved one with Down syndrome is five, twenty-five, forty-five, or older, there are still actions you can take to manage their health risks. Start by familiarizing yourself, other family members and caregivers, and your self-advocate with the six common health risks. And most critically, ensure your self-advocate's primary care doctor and specialists are aware of the prevalence of these conditions and why and how they should be monitored and addressed for your family.

Many larger cities offer Down syndrome, transition, or special needs clinics or hospitals that specialize in these needs and typically offer exceptional service. See the National Down Syndrome Congress' clinic listing in our resource section. However, many families may not have access to such care, so it is essential that you research your medical team, test their knowledge, educate them with information, and ensure their dedication to providing your self-advocate with first-class medical attention. A medical team familiar with Down syndrome and common health risks is more likely to properly diagnose issues than mainstream medicine.

Identifying and treating common health issues does more than extend lifespan—it improves the quality of life for your loved one. In many cases, early intervention of common conditions can make a huge difference in your self-advocate's health, future burdens, and overall independence.

Chaya and her mother, Thora, share their illuminating story of challenge and discovery as a family with Down syndrome and autism.

Family Feature
Chaya's Story

Our entire philosophy in raising Chaya has been: accommodate, accommodate, accommodate. She has always been an independent person and we believe our job is to find ways to allow her to do things for herself.

The challenges that have come up are due, not only to Down syndrome, but the fact that Chaya is autistic as well. This dual diagnosis is rare enough that we have often felt alone and found ourselves fighting the systems in place to help because their understanding of each diagnosis is distinct and separate, yet the combination is often misunderstood. We've had to educate many people and their backing organizations on how the two overlap and how that presents in Chaya, specifically. We are by no means experts on

Down syndrome or the dual presentation of Down syndrome with autism. We are experts on Chaya, though!

At fifteen years old, she is an exuberant light who shines love, care, and empathy on everyone she meets! She has a quick wit and a biting sense of humor that will first surprise you and then delight you. Chaya is smart and loves reading in general. Lately it's been anatomy books. She wants to be a biologist and study the human body. There's no doubt in our minds that she could, given her determination and self-awareness.

Our job is to nurture that and guide her to grow and become an independent adult. When she was young, maybe three or four years old, she started that toddler stage. You know the one, where "I do myself!" and she just never stopped. We knew pretty quickly that we needed to be building and stacking her skills. So, with the help of her teachers and therapists, we began working toward the necessary skills that would eventually become reading. Chaya always loved books and we knew reading would open a door to so many things for her.

We read to her every day and picked a letter for her to identify whenever she saw it. She would get so excited when she'd find the letter 'D' and sound out, "Dee! dee!" We'd pick harder and harder letters to say until she was able to make sounds of them together and she was off. It wasn't long before she was reading basic words and then books.

We did this with every evolving skill. When we saw an area in which she was struggling, we'd try skill stacking and when it didn't look like it was going to work, we started thinking of accommodations. Brushing teeth is a great example: her fine motor skills weren't there yet, and we didn't want her to give up, so we found a wide-handled electric toothbrush that required minimal fine motor control and taught her to use it. She was so proud to be brushing her own teeth! The toothpaste mess was another story! In fact, we found a toothpaste product that comes in single "serving" bites so she can chew to release it and that's how we avoid cleaning the bathroom twice a day, haha.

These days, Chaya has a system for pretty much everything. I think that's thanks to the autistic need for routine. Her day includes getting up and watching her favorite show for a bit, then she comes upstairs, takes her medicine, makes breakfast and gets ready for the day. She's learning to count and use money and to find things at the grocery store using the signs to guide her. It won't be long before she's almost entirely independent and able to do whatever she wants with her days. She's trying to convince us to give her the house once she turns eighteen. Maybe not whatever she wants, haha!

Thora, Chaya's mom

SECTION III — FOUNDATIONS FOR THE FUTURE

Chapter 8
Financial & Legal

Too many people are unaware of all the financial resources available for their family. Others feel fortunate to have adequate income and believe public assistance is not for them. I'll tell you right now, **no matter how you define it, independence is expensive.**

If your self-advocate lives at home for an extra decade or two, that creates about 25 percent greater costs than you likely anticipated. When a new home is in order, all options are costly, ranging from $500 to $5,000 per month or more. Hence, it's not a surprise that poverty within the I/DD community is twice as prevalent as the general public, due largely to lower income potential and higher needs.[61] Public assistance is woefully inadequate but can still serve as a tangible resource. You should know your options and how and when to get all the resources due your family.

Every time I talk to parents, we discover available resources that they are just not aware of. It's no wonder. There is a wide variety programs sponsored by many different agencies, and no single list is handed to parents when your child is born or turns eighteen. Recognizing this complicated and confusing array, some families adopt the mantra that "ignorance is bliss," preferring not to open this Pandora's box. However, failure to address these services *will* cost you hundreds of thousands of dollars. Starting early helps ease the burden.

Your first step is reading this guidebook and working through the associated free, online worksheets to help understand what independence means to your family, including what that may cost and how you can pay for that investment.

A few small-print items:
1. States and even counties can offer different benefits, so check your local agencies.
2. I'm not a financial planner but I've compiled this chapter with heavily researched data, along with input and review by two highly qualified benefits advisors, Barbara Bush[62] and Thomas Kroehle.[63]
3. I'm not a lawyer; however, I am a parent who has participated in many sessions with planners focusing on resources for families with disabilities and have engaged with experts to ensure I'm bringing you the best information available.

For those outside the US, your country may have some similar programs but the specifics that follow will not apply. Seek local resources for your Independence Plan.

There is a lot of information to follow so I will break it down simply and recap life cycle actions at the end. Let's first understand how Social Security programs are organized and what each may provide. We will then address requirements to start and maintain eligibility. This will include some important risks and tips to avoid so you don't inadvertently breach the rules and void benefit eligibility. Then we will cover legal structures including guardianship, ABLE accounts, wills and special needs trusts, and more.

Social Security Programs

For our discussions, we will break Social Security programs into two categories: federal and state. Each has an income and medical/services component. Each has its own rules for eligibility.

You are likely familiar with the federally managed Social Security retirement system that most everyone pays into while working and can draw from later in life. Your loved one with Down syndrome can benefit from various aspects of this federal program, as well as state managed benefits. It is incumbent upon you to understand what each program entails, how your self-advocate may be eligible, and how to ensure they maintain that eligibility. For our purposes, I'm providing a general primer that scratches below the surface and raises critical awareness. I recommend you consult a financial advisor or someone who specializes in benefits for the disabled community in order to understand specific nuances of long-term planning for your family.

	Financial	Medical & Services
Federally managed	• SS Retirement • SS Disability • SS Survivorship	• Medicare
State-managed	• Supplemental Security Income	• Medicaid/HIPP • Social Services (waiver programs)

Federally Managed Programs

Self-Advocate's Own Disability Insurance

Your self-advocate may qualify for their own Social Security Disability Insurance (SSDI). If your disabled child is deemed disabled before age twenty-two and their gross earnings are approximately $1,640 (for 2023) or more per month in three consecutive months, they will earn one credit. They generally need one-and-a-half years of works or six credits to qualify for their own Social Security Disability Insurance. However, satisfying this threshold may jeopardize SSI/Medicaid benefits as described in the next section. Consult with a financial planner well-versed in special needs instruments to understand the tradeoffs within your long-term plan.

Parent-Related Benefits (Retirement, Survivors, Disability)

This federal program applies to Americans who pay into the Social Security system. Often spouses as well as children (up to age eighteen) of those who are retired, disabled, or deceased also receive benefits. However, in these instances, if the child is disabled or for our purposes has Down syndrome, such benefits, termed Retirement, Survivors, and Disability Insurance (RSDI), may continue for the child's lifetime if certain eligibility requirements are met and maintained.

In these circumstances, your self-advocate may be eligible for 50 percent of the retired or disabled parent's monthly Social Security benefits, subject to a family maximum. That portion increases to 75 percent of the Social Security benefits of the parent upon the parent's death. Given the extended lifespan of adults with Down syndrome, these benefits can add up to a significant amount of money.

Consider a common scenario of a parent retiring at sixty and receiving Social Security benefits of $2,000 per month, who later dies at eighty. If their child with Down syndrome is thirty at the time of their parent's retirement and lives to the age of sixty themselves, their benefits would total $420,000. This amount will vary based on timing and the parent's Social Security–associated earnings. In any case, the impact to your loved one's resources is considerable.

To qualify, your loved one with Down syndrome must remain "connected" to their parent's Social Security accounts. This is accomplished first by presenting documentation of disability and second by showing that the child with Down syndrome does not earn enough income themselves, i.e., does not exceed the substantial gainful activity (SGA), which is $1,470 per month for 2023. If your self-advocate earns over the SGA amount more than any two months, the link with their parents Social Security account is severed, with little chance of reinstatement.

Depending on the amount of the Retirement, Survivors, and Disability Insurance (RSDI) benefit your loved one with Down syndrome receives, they may no longer collect their own SSI. (We'll discuss this in the state-managed section below.) This is okay. Social Security must pay you the most you are entitled to receive but not the cumulative of both RSDI and SSI.

Medicare Benefits

Medicare covers many of the costs associated with hospital stays, doctor visits, laboratory costs, medical supplies and equipment, home health care and prescription costs for people aged sixty-five and over. However, your disabled adult child (DAC) may qualify for Medicare twenty-four months after receiving RSDI or SSDI, regardless of age.

State-Managed Programs

Supplemental Security Income (SSI)

This is a federal program managed at the state level. Upon your child's eighteenth birthday, the Social Security Administration only considers the child's income and not the parents' when determining benefits eligibility. Qualification for SSI is based on two criteria: a diagnosis of a severe disability and assurance that the individual does not earn over a threshold amount as described below.

Social Security requests original diagnosis and chromosome testing, medical records from doctors seen for the disability in the last five years, and the most recent IEP, ARD and FIE (Full Individual Evaluation) documentation to satisfy the first criteria. They may also want a current psychological evaluation done in the last six months to one year.

Regarding financial status, find out the typical monthly SSI benefits in your state. (In 2023, it's $914 per month in most states, and is updated annually in October based on cost-of-living adjustments. If your self-advocate earns more than that amount anytime in the twelve months *before applying* for SSI benefits, it will be very difficult to get approved for SSI because your self-advocate has shown they have a capacity to earn a substantial wage. You will need several different forms and supporting documents to file for SSI.

Once Social Security has approved the person financially, they will send the application to Disability Determination Services, which will determine if the disability is severe enough to prevent your child from earning a substantial wage (equivalent to the SGA amount or approximately $1,470 on a consistent basis) in the future. This process can take three to nine months, depending on the workload of each agency. Once the application is approved, your disabled adult child's benefit will begin from the date the SSI application was filed. The process may be cumbersome, but people with Down syndrome generally qualify if they have not breached the financial limits above.

Once the application is approved, Social Security will determine if the disabled adult child is paying their fair share of living expenses. If not, they will reduce the benefit by one-third ($304.67 in 2023). To receive the maximum SSI benefit available, your child must pay his fair share of household expenses. A simple rental agreement should be signed by both the parent (landlord) and the child (renter).

Gwendolyn was unable to secure the full amount of SSI until we opened an ABLE account for her. (We'll cover ABLE accounts later in this chapter.) I deposited $600 per month into her ABLE account. The administrator of the ABLE account, my wife, then paid me $600 per month from the ABLE account.

Once you have two months of rent being paid, you can submit SSA Form 8006, the copy of the rental agreement, and a copy of the ABLE account showing the rent amount has been withdrawn monthly, to the SSA office. This may sound silly, but it is a legal structure which may support the full SSI benefit.

<u>Earnings Limit</u>

Once your loved one is receiving SSI, it is critical that you monitor and manage their income and assets in order to maintain eligibility. If their earnings exceed $1,913 (2023) in any given month, they lose their SSI for that month. If they do that for nine consecutive months, then they may lose their determination of disability. This could mean they no longer qualify for their SSI, and that they also are no longer connected to their parent's SSA work record. Their disability status may only be reinstated under a different diagnosis in the future. Talk with a Social Security Disability expert before this happens to consider alternatives and impacts.

Frequency of paycheck receipt can make a difference. Is your self-advocate paid once or twice per month or every two weeks? If paid monthly, you should have a clear understanding of their earnings per month. However, if they are paid every two weeks then, depending on the calendar, they could receive three paychecks in a month, i.e., November 1, 15, 29. This would result in greater earnings in that particular month, possibly exceeding allowable income.

If your self-advocate makes $15 per hour and works thirty hours a week and is paid every two weeks, they would earn $900 every two weeks. For months with only two pay periods, they would be okay ($1,800 earnings vs. the $1,913 monthly cap). However, if in this example there are three pay periods, they would gross $2,700 for that month and be over the allowed limit of $1,913, thus jeopardizing their SSI and the associated Medicaid coverage as well. Also, keep in mind any annual or holiday bonuses, which can also impact monthly earnings.

Asset Limit

Additionally, to maintain eligibility, your loved one's assets cannot exceed $2,000. An asset is anything that could be sold or used to pay for food and/or shelter:

- Money in their bank checking/savings account(s)
- Your self-advocate's credit card spending limit
- Any savings bonds in your loved one's name, perhaps purchased by a grandparent or others
- Other assets including stocks or bonds

You cannot just transfer any or all funds out of their bank account. Any transfers must be for *qualified expenses* such as food or shelter. (See www.ssa.gov for details.)

The SSI benefit can be deposited directly into an ABLE account (described later) if you are concerned that your self-advocate's checking account may go over the $2,000 limit. If your self-advocate has work income, you can avoid asset accumulation that could jeopardize their SSI eligibility by creating and using their ABLE account. If your loved one receives gifts, whether small birthday checks or larger proceeds from a relative's will, funds should be deposited either into an ABLE account (up to $17,000 contribution per calendar year) or a first-party special needs trust, also known as a self-settled special needs trust. We will cover these important instruments later in this chapter. These mechanisms will also protect the funds and your loved one's SSI and thus Medicaid eligibility. In other words, vehicles such as ABLE accounts, first-party special needs trusts and third-party special needs trusts are "protected," or not considered for asset calculation.

Finally, families should be aware that if your self-advocate one day meets that special someone and wants to get married, if both are I/DD and receive SSI benefits, the SSI income and assets caps are not doubled for the happy couple. The limits are reduced to only one and a half times the individual earnings or asset limits. Hence, there is a realistic chance both could lose SSI benefits or have to reduce their income accordingly. Also consider that when your self-advocate gets married, they are no longer connected to their parent's SSA work record. Consult a qualified benefits planner before considering official marriage certification.

Medicaid Benefits

Medicaid is a state-administered program and thus can vary by state. Generally, your child will be eligible at eighteen based on their diagnosis and qualification for SSI. If your self-advocate violates the income or asset SSI rules above, they will also lose Medicaid coverage.

Medicaid offers two programs you should be aware of:

- Primarily, Medicaid covers outpatient and inpatient medical and dental costs along with lab work, surgical services, nursing facilities, and residential support services such as occupational or speech therapy, all without a monthly premium. To benefit from this coverage, you need to see a professional who accepts Medicaid insurance. Medicaid also typically results in $0 prescriptions as well. If you have company-sponsored medical insurance, you can use it in tandem with Medicaid to ensure you pay the lowest co-pays for the widest range of services. In general, dependents are not eligible to stay on their parents' insurance beyond age twenty-six unless they have disabilities. Start the process early to gain this age waiver for your loved one by discussing with your employer's human resources department.

- Health Insurance Premium Payments (HIPP): Medicaid will also reimburse some or all of the parents' monthly medical (not dental) health insurance premiums if your child with disabilities is covered by that private insurance and has qualified for Medicaid. Thus, obtaining the age-waiver described above before your loved one turns 26 is imperative. This can apply not only while the parent is employed, but also if they receive company-sponsored medical insurance during their retirement. Generally, Medicaid will review eligibility each year and could decline or adjust based on cost. To learn more and apply, search for your state's HIPP program online. Estimated benefits vary

---

based on your monthly medical premiums, but this could amount to several hundred dollars per month or more.

<u>Social Services</u>

Each state's Medicaid program also includes social services, often called waiver programs. These typically include funding for respite care, home therapy, day programs, communication devices, mobility assistance such as walkers or wheelchairs, transportation, and housing costs. Each state manages their own programs. Thus, the names of the programs, eligibility, and funding amounts can vary considerably across the United States.

Every state has a budget with limited resources and a plethora of programs seeking a portion of that state budget. For Medicaid social services, states can generally be placed into one of two categories: cost cap-based or needs-based.

- **Cost cap** states, currently including California, Illinois, Massachusetts, provide limited services and funds to qualified families regardless of need and typically without a waiting list. However, the amount of benefits is limited because they theoretically serve every I/DD person in their state.

- **Needs-based** states usually involve a long waiting list that varies from a few years to well over a decade. However, once your name comes up, the state will award services and funding based on need so the proceeds can be significantly more, assisting with sizable day program and housing expenses thereafter.

It is critical that you understand the structure of your state's social services program. If you reside in a needs-based state, get on their waiting list(s) early—theoretically from day one!

Also, because given Medicaid services are state based, they do not transfer between states. Hence, if you move to another state, whether for a week or a decade, whether due to a work transfer or out of personal necessity, you will need to reapply for all the services (SSI, Medicaid, HIPP, and Social Services) in your new state. This will be a hassle and take time and may result in a gap in benefits. Most importantly, if you move to a needs-based state, you will have to get on their waiting list(s) for social services. When you move, you will be removed from your previous state's waiting list and will have to start over if you happen to return to that state, or even the same residence, in the future.

Each state may organize their services differently, with each program having its own applications, benefits, and waiting lists. Most states have two programs with separate application processes and waiting lists, where applicable:

Home living–type program: covers respite care, home care, and day program expenses

Home and community–based program: covers residential community costs.

States may offer other programs based on medical needs and financial standing. Spend time on your state's Medicaid website and visit them in person to understand all the programs they offer, which ones your self-advocate may qualify for, and how and when to apply. A handy website to get started is http://medicaidwaiver. org/state/vermont.html. Despite the name, this website provides a brief description of every state's program and their website links.

The Best State to Live In

Many parents are curious what are the best states to live in for services for their loved one with Down syndrome. This is a great question to ask, but not a simple one to answer. Most of the differences reside in the social services programs each state provides. Cost cap states may sound enticing because you get benefits much earlier. However, the reduced level of services and funding may leave you with a large bill to pay, especially if you anticipate your loved one will require a great deal of support, whether at home, through day programming, or with residential living.

If you are in a needs-based state, you don't want to invest your time riding a waitlist for years and then move to another needs-based state and start over. If you don't believe the cost cap service level will suffice, you may wish to be in a needs-based state early with the hope of getting off the waitlist and receiving benefits by the time your self-advocate is out of high school. Oftentimes, the best state for you to be in is the state you currently live in.

What is clear is that you will benefit from early planning. According to the report *A Place in the World*,[64] only 17 percent of adults with I/DD receive Medicaid funding for social services or long-term support services. This is due in part to long waiting lists but largely because of a lack of awareness of the programs and application process.

Non–Social Security State Programs

The US Department of Agriculture's Food and Nutrition Services offers the Supplemental Nutrition Assistance Program (SNAP) through each state. This program, known as food stamps in the past, is available for those who receive SSI and meet other income and cost bases. Visit https://www.fns.usda.gov/snap/ state-directory to find your state's SNAP website for information and application. Benefits vary based on the child's income and expenses, ranging from $100 per month to thousands. Benefits are received in the form of a debit card anyone in the family can use to purchase grocery items.

Legal Considerations

It's important to understand legal documents that can protect your self-advocate's benefits and independence. This section describes each instrument and how and when to proceed. I suggest you consult an attorney who specializes in legal documents for those with I/DD to ensure your family is properly safeguarded.

Guardianship

At the age of eighteen, your children legally become adults and are able to make decisions for themselves, including financial, medical, and residential decisions. Guardianship judges often prefer that the family try a less restrictive way to support your self-advocate before seeking guardianship. Review your options below and advocate for the solution that best fits your family's needs.

There are two documents you may consider short of guardianship: supported decision-making agreement or a medical power of attorney. These documents allow your adult child to seek your advice and include you in all legal and medical decisions. However, both documents depend on your self-advocate always inviting you into the room and taking counsel from you. If they disagree with you, these documents have no power. What's worse, if it appears your loved one is not capable of making necessary decisions, rather than consulting you, the other party, such as a hospital or school administrator, will bring in state resources to act on your self-advocate's behalf.

Imagine your loved one needs to converse with a doctor to decide on a course of treatment or surgery. Consider your self-advocate making financial decisions that may impact the complex topics of SSI, Medicaid, or social service benefits discussed in this chapter. What if your loved one wishes to drive or get married? If you have guardianship, you have the *right* to be in the room to provide counsel to your self-advocate and ultimately to make the prudent decision for them if they can't or won't. If you don't have guardianship, doctors, lawyers, teachers, or others legally cannot allow you in the room unless your self-advocate maintains either a supported decision-making document or medical power of attorney and allows you to be present.

I am a huge proponent for person-centered planning and for every self-advocate's involvement and voice. However, **you must ask yourself if you are confident they will make well thought-out decisions in crucial and complex situations. If you hesitate, I suggest you obtain legal guardianship.** You may still involve your self-advocate, ensure they understand the questions, and give them every opportunity to provide input, but ultimately you make the decisions. The independence journey as depicted in this book, and especially in this section, has many complex parts. It is a lot to absorb to ensure your self-advocate and their independence is protected. **Don't let their eighteenth birthday approach without considering the issue of guardianship for your family.** Who do you think is best prepared to make these decisions?

My wife and I enlisted the services of a lawyer well-versed in legal documents and guardianship for the I/DD community and we secured legal guardianship when Gwendolyn turned eighteen. It took several months and some investment to complete the process. We also must renew her guardianship annually with a small fee. We always have the right to change our mind but remain confident in our decision.

One footnote: you may consider preserving your self-advocate's right to vote during the initial guardianship process. This may require your doctor to sign off on a particular level of mental capacity and is ultimately determined by the judge.

ABLE Account

An ABLE account is a 529A savings account for individuals with a disability that occurred prior to age twenty-six. The account can receive up to $17,000 per year (in 2023) of income but contributions can also be considerably higher if the beneficiary works and earns income while not participating in his or her employer's retirement plan.[65] Lifetime maximum contributions vary by state but can go as high as $500,000[66] with up to $100,000 in the ABLE account exempt from the SSI $2,000 individual asset limit described earlier.

The ABLE account does not impact your child's SSI or Medicaid eligibility if deposits remain within the stated limits. Anyone can contribute to the ABLE account. Though this is most often used as a short-term vehicle for protecting assets and SSI/Medicaid eligibility, you can opt to invest portions of the ABLE account savings if you wish.

If there are funds in the ABLE account and your child dies, Medicaid is to be paid back for anything they have spent on your self-advocate through remaining ABLE proceeds. If there are any funds left afterward, they can be distributed to the person(s) designated in your self-advocate's will.

You must use the ABLE funds for specific, but wide-ranging, costs including housing, transportation, and most living expenses. There may be tax benefits as well. Most ABLE accounts are set up through the state comptroller's office. You can only have one ABLE account at a time. You can shop around on the internet without having to reside in the state in which your ABLE account is based. ABLE accounts are basically all the same, but do check details before signing up.

Last Will and Testament and Special Needs Trusts

When your loved one with Down syndrome is born, you should consult an attorney who specializes in I/DD issues to either update your last will and testament or establish a new will. If you direct funds toward your self-advocate without considering I/DD limits, you could severely curtail their eligibility for public benefits.

A special needs trust is a legal document that enables you and your family to direct funds to your child or adult with Down syndrome without risking their eligibility for Medicaid or Social Security. When you talk with your attorney, discuss the different types of trusts and the tax implications when leaving money to your self-advocate.

If you anticipate that grandparents or others, upon their death, may leave funds to your loved one, you might want to establish a separate trust. Your attorney will provide you wording to share with others who may consider gifting your child legacy money in the future, so their generosity doesn't have unintended consequences.

If a divorce occurs in the family, any child support provided for the child's benefit past the age of eighteen is considered the disabled child's income and may disqualify them from SSI and Medicaid benefits. The divorce decree must provide language approved by the family law court to direct child support to the first-party special needs trust and not to the attorney general's office. Any money in the child's name after age eighteen must be deposited into this type of a trust to avoid SSI/Medicaid disqualification. Again note, the first beneficiary of this trust is Medicaid.

Many families assume all special needs trusts are the same. However, there are a wide variety of trusts that serve different purposes to protect your self-advocate and family. Be sure to consult an expert for proper protection.

Documentation

Besides the above legal instruments, consider two additional items: a letter of intent and a home filing system.

A proper letter of intent (LOI) may be the most important document you have. It is not a legal document, but it directs future guardians, caregivers, or executors on how to care for your loved one if/when you are not able to do so. You may note your loved one's likes and dislikes, allergies, school or work aspirations, current benefits, and experts that future caregivers should engage with to ensure your loved one's rights and resources are protected. You can find many LOI templates online or through your financial or legal planners.

Finally, be sure you maintain a detailed filing system either in your home office or online. Carefully organize and maintain documents ranging from medical diagnosis, medical issues and tests, financial benefits, public services provided, school ARD/IEP documentation, and proof of income and assets. These will help you answer any questions if requested by the state or federal Social Security Administration, assist you in applying for additional benefits, and direct future guardians or caregivers to prudently manage your loved one's medical, financial, and legal journey.

Call to Action

As the parent/guardian, you will need to make many decisions with your self-advocate about their future. **Do you feel confident their housing, day program, living expenses, and other needs can be provided for through their lifelong employment with the family covering any potential shortfall?** If not, you should be diligent in applying for and maintaining all public benefits while protecting these benefits through proper legal instruments.

Regardless of your loved one's age, the information in this chapter is a lot to absorb. As the parent or guardian, the responsibilities are yours. It can be a heavy load, but now that you are familiar with each resource, you can place them into the proper buckets based on timing and then return to each when needed.

Timing	Focus
At birth	• State SSI Social Services (Medicaid waivers) • Legal will & testament and special needs trust • Documentation filing system • Letter of intent
Before starting first employment	• State SSI limitations to preserve SSI/RSDI • ABLE account
At 18	• State SSI, Medicaid • HIPP, SNAP • Guardianship or alternative • Letter of intent (updated)
Later—event specific	• Move into residence-State SSI/Medicaid and Medicaid Social Services (waiver programs) • Relocation-State SSI/Medicaid and Medicaid Social Services (waiver programs) • Self-advocate marriage-State SSI/Medicaid • Parent retirement/disability/death-Federal SS

The challenges before you are unique. Lean on professionals that have the expertise to guide you through these encounters. Your self-advocate's future depends on it.

Encourage your local Down syndrome association to host a benefits planner, financial planner, and attorney well versed in disability rights and benefits to get the latest information and to identify professionals who may assist your own family's journey.

Family Feature
Your Story

This chapter's **Family Feature** is YOU! So often we can get dragged down by the sheer immensity of parenting our loved one with Down syndrome. And after the last couple of chapters, that weight may feel heavier than usual. But I invite you to step back and celebrate!

You have undoubtedly done a fantastic job navigating the unexpected challenges life has presented thus far in steering your family in the right direction. And now you have picked up *The Essential Guide* and completed over half this guidebook. You are gaining insights on vital information that will change the trajectory of your family and your loved one in particular. It may feel overwhelming at times, but it is important to have eyes wide open, to be aware of the challenges and opportunities, and then to plan and take actions accordingly. And you are doing just that. Congratulations!

While reading the full Guide will raise your awareness and vision for the future, you can also use each section's plans and actions and the downloadable Independence Plan to lend focus on specific actions for each stage of life.

This is a lifelong journey. While it is essential to develop and see the whole plan, the true difference is in accomplishing bite-size pieces along the way.

Revel in your successes and dedication.

You are now writing your own Family Feature!

I'd love to hear from you. Share your **Family Feature** with me at BeyondDownSyndrome@gmail.com and I may post it on my website.

SECTION IV
TAKING ON THE WORLD

High school graduation is a landmark moment for every family. We may feel frustrated at times that the public school system does not always deliver what we argue for in annual IEPs and ARDs, but our self-advocates are exposed to a lot of information in school. They not only may learn to read and write, do math and tell time, but they are challenged to practice and grow these skills most every day. Additionally, they have the chance to socialize with classmates, integrate with the general population, and communicate with authority figures. It may be hard to identify such developments day-by-day, but if you reflect on your self-advocates' abilities and confidence in these areas several years ago, you will likely recognize astounding growth.

When the school guardrails disappear, parents often feel like they are falling off a cliff, with no clear direction or options. Families tend to go one of two directions:

1. The self-advocate spends considerably more time at home and often loses some of the educational and social skills developed in high school.

2. The self-advocate and parents reach out to create new opportunities. This guidebook is intended to help you navigate the choices and steps to create such possibilities.

This section focuses on opportunities largely outside the home. This exposure helps bridge the sizeable gap between self-sufficiency at home within the comfort of the family unit and broadening the self-advocate's independence within the community at large. Operating outside the home requires further skill development and courage for the self-advocate, and another level of "letting go" for the parents and caregivers.

Post-high school presents an important transition for families. Either the path for growth continues and even expands as the self-advocate shifts out of the classroom and into society, or it gets stunted, oftentimes leading to regression of the skills and confidence your loved one and the family have worked so hard to establish over the years.

Section IV: Plans and Actions		
#	Action	Life Stage*
1	Consider post–high school continuing ed options	Adolescence
2	Determine if primary subsistence is from work or public benefits	Before Employment
3	Calculate monthly work earnings that maintain benefits	Before Employment
4	Utilize resources and self-directed employment searches	Before Employment

If your loved one has passed this stage but has not completed this action, place this at the top of your action plan

Check out resources and references at the back of the book. Downloads are available for free at:
http://www.beyonddownsyndrome.net/The-Essential-Guide

Chapter 9
Continuing Education

Education, whether public, private, or homeschooling, absorbs considerable time and energy for the family during your loved one's first eighteen to twenty-two years. This is the breeding ground for independence as they learn academics, life skills, and social engagement. Learning should be a priority both during their formal education and beyond.

Formal Education

It's quite important to set short and long-term goals starting from childhood. What do you and your self-advocate want to achieve this academic year? More importantly, what are your longer term Independent Plan objectives? It may be hard to fathom, but it is worthwhile to consider their future adult life.

Do you envision your self-advocate working, taking transportation by themselves, living alone or within a community? Share these goals with your schoolteachers and administration through the annual ARD and IEP. Create annual goals that support the long-term vision. The many aspects of this guidebook shouldn't wait until they are eighteen. Align yourself with the school staff in promoting these skills for your self-advocate and then hold them accountable.

And Beyond...

Our loved ones have a longer runway. While it often takes a while to develop certain skills, **they have an awesome opportunity to keep learning well beyond their teens.** If we provide the right support and exposure, they will continue to develop and grow. There is no reason the step changes that astound us throughout their first two decades won't continue...as long as we create some form of continuing education beyond high school years. If we fail to do that, not only will their learning curve slump, but regression will be the result.

Regression Syndrome

Dr. Brian Chicoine of the Adult Down Syndrome Center at the Advocate Medical Group in Park Ridge, Illinois, speaks often about the potential decline in the skills of people with Down syndrome. He calls the extreme version of this regression syndrome.[67] His experience has found that many people with Down syndrome lose skills due to medical conditions, traumas, or familial or social changes. Each must be assessed in their own right, leading to appropriate adjustments or cognitive, speech, occupational, or physical therapies as necessary to return skills and growth.

The often traumatic post-high school shift can cause this type of regression. **A change of scenery, a loss of social interaction, the elimination of structured reading, writing, or math time, or a reduction of life skills teachings can all happen when high school comes to an end.** Hence, it is no surprise that some adults with Down syndrome slowly lose social skills, reading skills, or the ability to take care of themselves, as well as the initiative to learn new things and develop accordingly. With the schoolteacher removed from the equation, parents assume this role by default.

In our first **Family Feature** for this chapter, Heather shares her stepdaughter Ayla's regression due to the COVID pandemic and their arduous road back.

You may not realize the many roles that have transferred to you. You may not have the skills or time available to continue to teach your self-advocate in order to avoid a decline in skills or, as Dr. Chicoine terms more severe cases, regression syndrome.

However, it is essential to address this gap, in one or both of the following ways:

1. Parent-directed activities (in essence, parents become the homeschooling teacher)
2. Structured programs arranged to provide the stimulus and exposure to keep your self-advocate growing and moving forward

To avoid regression syndrome, it's important our self-advocates do not settle into a plateau but rather continue to practice what they know and learn new skills to grow. The education and learning phase of their life does not end after high school—it simply transfers to a different arena.

Post–High School Options

There are several styles of post–high school programs to consider. Respondents to our UPL Family Survey indicated that the most popular approaches were college programs (9 percent), day programs (24 percent), and stay at home options (67 percent):

1. Inclusive college programs: Every year more universities are creating inclusive programs for those with I/DD. Options range from local community college classes that

can be taken either online or in-person while living at home to the full college experience—living on campus and taking classes toward a degree. You can find a long, but not exhaustive, list of such programs at https://www.ivywise. com/ivywise-knowledgebase/resources/article/colleges-with-programs-for-students-with-special-needs/. These programs tend to be for the more independent students but are not limited to starting at a particular age. Perhaps your child would be best prepared for such a program at age twenty or twenty-five? In either case, if this is of interest to your self-advocate, do lots of homework. Understand the environment they will live in, the classes they may take, and the academic and social support they will receive along the way. Through online investigation, on-campus tours and meetings, and discussions with other families currently or previously enrolled, you can determine if this option is best for your self-advocate. It is indeed important to stretch their mind and comfort zone, but not to place them in a strange environment without the proper support and security. Clemson University offers one of the more established and well-known inclusive programs. They describe their program and philosophy in one of the articles shared at the end of this chapter.

2. Day programs: Day programs come in all shapes and sizes. The variety of options is tremendous and warrants a lot of research. Some programs are half days and others full days for one to five days per week. They may offer transportation to/from the program or be affiliated with a residential living community (covered in section V). Some provide classroom-like settings with life skills and

vocational teaching as well as field practice. Most programs provide ample opportunity for social interaction during the day, while some also offer nighttime or weekend dances and family outings. With highly skilled teachers and classes focused on each participants' abilities, needs, and interests, this style of learning can boost skills and confidence. However, some programs are embarrassingly weak. They plant their attendees at long tables in a warehouse with paper and color pencils and very little oversight or challenge. Participants might make products like flowers, jewelry, or pottery, which the program then sells. This can be a great skill-building method that instills pride in the resident. However, there is a fine line between developing skills and pride and basically creating a slave-labor situation with quotas and expectations. Some of these programs do pay the participants out of the proceeds and others do not, all while you pay tuition for the program itself. Be sure to do your homework and visit your short list. Observe sessions in progress. Use the amenities and considerations (chapter 13) as well as the research and questions list (chapter 14) provided for residential living options to find and evaluate day programs in your area. Talk to other parents. Ask if your self-advocate can attend a trial day or week to see if it is the right fit. There is a wide disparity within this category. Some may spark further learning, while others aren't any better than adult babysitting. Depending on the program, your state benefits may pay for some or all of the cost to attend. Be sure to ask the administrators about this and see the financial resources chapter for more details on applying for such benefits for your self-advocate. Ms. Calista Boyd, former head teacher at Houston's Friends of Down Syndrome's academy describes a benchmark program in another story at the end of this chapter.

3. Homeschooling: If your self-advocate does not participate in either a college or day program, then home is likely their base. The responsibility will lie with you to create a homeschooling-style curriculum for your child. This does not have to be a nine-to-five, five-day-a-week formal program. Mainly, expose your self-advocate to new experiences and grow skills like reading and writing, life skills, social skills, and independence rather than have them just sit around all day. Certainly, a work program, described in the next chapter, may also be an important part of your self-advocate's day. If your loved one stays at home, parents generally initiate all activities. This homeschooling approach is not for everyone. Over the years, many parents have enjoyed respite during the day. Acting as their primary teacher requires time, patience, and initiative. Consider how you can fulfill these areas through some scheduled time and outings that you create. Daniel's mom, Carolyn, surmises, "Everything can foster independence as the young person is getting out and interacting with others, learning new skills, and all the social nuances that go with it. The challenge is finding what is out there and getting things started [yourself] if there is not anything." Reflect on the hobbies section of chapter 3 for other ideas. Carolyn assesses many "young adults who live at home have very full and engaging lives. Their parents make it a priority."

However, if you conclude this is not a role you wish to play beyond nights and weekends, consider the day programs or college programs in your area.

Regardless of which educational option best serves your family, keep in mind that the college experience will end. Even the most vibrant homeschooling program will come to an end either when your self-advocate needs more, or when you are no longer able to provide such an experience as age catches up with us all. Carolyn shares, "Everyone is going to get old and maybe not be as healthy and active as we are now. I encourage [Daniel] to move out. If something happens to me (or his dad) and he is still at home, the impact will be even more devastating to him, especially if I am his everything."

What will your next step be? Perhaps your current program is the perfect catalyst for your loved one's growth now but **always keep an eye toward the future to avoid the unexpected.**

Lifelong learning is an essential component of your self-advocate's success. This chapter offers three features to provide broadening perspectives:

1. Heather shares a traumatic story of her stepdaughter's regression as she lost her independence during the COVID-19 pandemic, and the brave love the family provided to find a path back for Ayla.

2. Ms. Boyd, of the Friends of Down Syndrome, shares the philosophy behind a truly unique day program in Houston.

3. Dr. Joe Ryan, executive director at Clemson University, describes the ClemsonLIFE inclusive college program.

Family Feature
Ayla's Story

Through The Storm: Ayla's Journey

Something was happening to my stepdaughter, Ayla, in the fall of 2020. I had been a part of her life since she was six. Suddenly at thirty, this previously confident and imaginative spirit, who was mentally operating at around age seventeen, could no longer complete tasks on her chore board. She could not complete sentences. Her stammering, which had been intermittent, was constant. She would freeze in place, staring into space. When she would walk, it would be like a robot— backing up, making squares in the kitchen with her steps to move only a few feet to the sink or refrigerator. She seemed agitated, then somber. She lost interest in social media, even her phone. Showers, where she had been completely independent, she could no longer complete on her own. Once a spry and energetic swimmer placing at Special Olympic events, she feared water touching her.

By the spring of 2021, her personality morphed into one of defiance and tantrums. She lost awareness of time. In washing her hands, she would run the sink until water spilled over, ruining cabinets below. Her hygiene worsened. Shampoo and hand soap warning labels frightened her. Incontinence and fogginess emerged. She began lying about completing her morning basics. She used to take pride in walking our greyhounds one at a time. She could no longer walk them alone. Eating meals took two times longer. When taking pills or drinking water, Ayla would make choking sounds until we looked at her. Ayla reacted the opposite of what was asked, and skills she had as a young girl were gone. Ayla was fast becoming an invalid.

Her mom, Karen, her father, Ray, and I continually searched for reasons why this had happened, and so quickly. Ayla's mom, Karen, shared her fear that had crossed our minds, "Did Ayla have early dementia?" Tests, evaluations, psychiatry, and psychology appointments were made. Ayla's social worker, Stephanie, reassured us—no dementia. Behavioral and chemical were the next considerations. Ayla received antidepressants and antianxiety medications based on what they observed in sessions and from our feedback.

During one conversation with Ayla, I gained a little clue as to her regression. "What do you feel when you are doing these things?" I asked.

"Feath [Ayla's endearing name for me, short for Feather], I feel like I'm in a storm and can't get to you or Dad. I can't turn off the storm." Her issues persisted. Ayla spent time with Ray and me in Florida, and in Virginia with her mom and stepdad. At one of her psychiatrist sessions, she repeated the same sentence: "I'm in a storm." As the months and year passed, we shared experiences with Ayla in each household. Ray noticed that Ayla would turn her behaviors on and off. In public, at restaurants and shops, she would wave to people, smile, say hello without stammering. We would get home, and she would robot, stammer, and act defiant.

More than anything, parents wish to see their children develop into their best possible selves, to tap into their truest desires…to be happy. Ayla had lost her independence, her ability to contribute to her family and others. COVID shut the world down and when the world came out of hiding, the post-COVID world did not include the opportunities that previously cultivated Ayla's confidence. Even if those opportunities would emerge, Ayla had regressed to the point she could not take part in them.

It was now 2022, and Ayla was in full regression, acting at times like a four-year-old. We shared these observations with her social worker, Stephanie. "I've known Ayla since she was very young," Stephanie began. "Ayla has ALWAYS wanted to be independent. She has enjoyed helping the family and took pride in her jobs at Books-A-Million and Domino's. She used to stay at home on her own after high school, prior to getting her jobs. Now, her mom is not working, Ray retired, and Heather's career ended recently. COVID suspended Ayla's jobs, and Special Olympics ceased due to the pandemic. All Ayla's outlets for independence are severed."

Ray and I realized, with Stephanie's outside perspective, that Ayla had lost what Ayla loved most—being independent and on her own. Ayla was unable to articulate her disappointment and frustration. What she could control was getting attention, and unruly behavior was getting her plenty of attention. We shared this realization with Karen and her husband.

In the months to follow, we focused on behavior modification tactics recommended by Stephanie and others. When Ayla behaved badly, we would call her out on the action. At first, it felt harsh, to correct Ayla with every move. Initially Ayla met our "re-training" with continued opposite behavior. We stayed consistent. If she could not wash her face, then she could not choose her own clothes. If she could not eat properly, she lost TV privileges. This upset Ayla because her ability to choose for herself was being threatened by her behavior.

When she returned to Karen's house, Ayla's bad behaviors resulted in discussions and corrective actions similar to the actions Ray and I initiated. We all shared tips on what worked and what did not. We would vent to each other.

Over two years into this journey with Ayla, we are seeing signs of the old Ayla, the pre-COVID Ayla. We share numerous details with her doctors, therapists, and Stephanie. Friends have helped us in reestablishing acceptable behavior for Ayla. They invite us all over for meals or activities where Ayla must interact with others, both familiar and unfamiliar. Karen, Ray, and I continue to help Ayla improve through increased structure, clear and simple expectations, and other tools to help modify her behavior. While there is still frustration at times, we have a plan that is working to restore Ayla.

Special Olympics has resumed. Ayla is more chipper and more active daily. She wears an activity tracker, and competes for steps with Karen, Ray, and me. As a united front, we are challenging Ayla to restore the skills and discipline needed to hold a job again.

Recently we experienced a breakthrough moment. After a particularly tough evening, where Ayla acted out enough to earn her a "corner sit/time out," she apologized for her behavior. Never had she done that! We could see our old Ayla, working through that "storm." Ayla recognizes what makes her Ayla, and we are all pulling for her to make the days ahead her most joyful days.

Heather, Ayla's stepmom

Expert Advice
Ms. Boyd's Story

Friends of Down Syndrome
Lifelong Education & Learning

My name is Calista Boyd and I have been teaching all ages from preschool to college remedial reading over the past forty years. I enjoyed teaching and most of all I enjoy watching the students achieve their goals and become successful adults. In the last fourteen years, I have worked with an amazing woman, Mrs. Rosa Rocha, who allowed me to use my skills and knowledge to teach adults with Down syndrome.

Through the years we addressed the needs of the students who came to us by developing unique educational and vocational programs at the Friends of Down Syndrome's academy. Our intent is to give them a jumpstart for their best life possible. We have over fifty students ranging from nineteen to sixty-nine attending our program in Houston.

Our program is based on the needs of the students. We aim to use their own skills to help them be lifetime learners and successful adults in the community. Our facility is bright and cheerful, clean, and welcoming to parents, visitors, and students.

Welcoming

When a student is considering enrolling, they are given a forty-five-minute evaluation through conversation, games, and directions. Each student is then placed into one of seven classes based on current skill set.

Prospective families are given a tour of the building so they can see the students in reading, math, social sciences, music, art, vocational, and exercise classes. The students always come up and say "hi" and shake their hand.

The unique hands-on, coordinated, and personalized approach has helped many adult students to read for the first time and for historically nonverbal students to speak at school and at home. The results have been remarkable.

Attendees fund their fees either themselves (privately) or through agencies and state benefits based on the number of days they attend each week.

Productive Days

Every day starts in the social hall with the Pledge of Allegiance and morning announcements. Routine helps students get in the learning mindset. Then each student goes to their schedule classes.

Each student learns differently, even with an all–Down syndrome program. Teachers utilize a variety of programs including Touch Math (a multi-sensory program), Raz-Kids (a computer reading program for school and home), and hands-on projects with microscopes, arts and crafts, and musical instruments. Additional classes on nutrition, physical education, speech, gardening, and vocational skills make our program quite unique. I have found that expression is their best way to communicate. I use the multisensory centers and personalized learning to help build verbal skills and confidence. The day ends with social time where students chat, dance, and sing. No time for boredom.

Culture

Respect and honesty for our fellow students and staff is mandatory. Behavioral issues are few and addressed swiftly through discussion, teaching, and reminders of the rules of respect.

Taking time to visit students one-on-one is both rewarding and impactful. Just having a cup of coffee or Coke and talking about their weekend, their dog, the goofy thing they did at the mall all build the rapport and trust necessary for everyone to succeed. And you'll have a friend forever.

Ms. Boyd, Retired FoDS lead teacher

There are currently 310 postsecondary education (PSE) programs located across forty-nine states. As the number of programs continues to expand it is important to identify a college program that best meets the individual needs of your son or daughter.

For the past thirteen years ClemsonLIFE (Learning Is for Everyone) has provided an inclusive collegiate experience that prepares young men and women with intellectual disabilities, ages eighteen to twenty-six, for competitive employment and independent living through a combination of academic coursework and career exploration. Approximately 55 percent of our students have Down syndrome.

ClemsonLIFE currently provides three different certificate programs, including the Basic Certificate Program, Advanced Certificate Program, and Hospitality Certificate Program.

Basic Certificate Program

Students in the basic program live on campus in four-bedroom apartments that are outfitted with a full kitchen and laundry area for students to practice independent living skills. Each apartment is comprised of three LIFE students and a traditional student. This independent living assistant (ILA) supervises the LIFE students during the evening and weekend hours, reinforcing the skills the students learned from their instructors during the week. LIFE students take a mixture of traditional and functional academic courses. The majority of coursework consists of functional academic modules focusing on independent living (e.g., banking, cleaning, transportation, shopping), employment (e.g., soft and hard skills), functional literacy/technology (e.g., emails), and health/wellness (e.g., hygiene, boundaries, relationships). Traditional courses are chosen based on personal interest (e.g., yoga).

Advanced Certificate Program

ClemsonLIFE also offers an advanced two-year program for students that have demonstrated the ability to safely live independently, sustain employment, and socially integrate during the basic program. These students move into apartments off campus without an independent living assistant but are monitored closely by a transition specialist as they practice independent living skills (e.g., cooking, cleaning, shopping, paying bills). The advanced program progresses with an increased emphasis on workplace experience, community integration, and independent living with transitionally reduced supports.

Hospitality Certificate Program

Hospitality certificate program students receive a combination of classroom and employment experiences to prepare them for employment in the hospitality industry (e.g., restaurants, hotels). This two-year program provides graduates with a ClemsonLIFE Hospitality Certificate while having the opportunity to receive other training/certifications (e.g., CPR/AED, hazmat, customer service).

Student Engagement

ClemsonLIFE students are active in the Clemson community participating in Greek life, student clubs, swim team, horseback riding, workout classes, sporting events, and more.

Employment Training

During the first year of study, students rotate through a series of month-long unpaid internships across four different employment settings (retail, food services, distribution center, hospitality industry) to assess individual employment skills and interests. During the second year of the program, students participate in paid employment both on and off campus. All students receive ongoing support and supervision from an employment instructor who provides a combination of classroom instruction and on-site job training.

Social Life

Throughout the PSE program, every student is paired with a traditional student who volunteers as a peer mentor. Mentors meet with students for at least an hour each week throughout the program. Students also attend social events with their mentors throughout the academic school year (e.g., bowling, dinner). Mentors and students work closely together to create achievable social and behavioral goals throughout the course of each semester. In addition to time spent with their mentor, all students participate in a variety of social activities (e.g., club activities, church affiliated events, lunch buddies, athletic events). Currently over a third of the PSE students are involved in Greek life fraternities and sororities, as well as other club opportunities on campus.

Physical and Mental Wellness

Exercise and nutrition strategies are embedded within the program to help foster lifelong healthy living. Students participate in five workout sessions each week that includes a combination of both group activities (e.g., Zumba), as well as individual physical workout sessions (e.g., lifting, swimming). Students also participate in ninety minutes of nutrition classes each week that encourage healthy eating. In addition, a mental health counselor provides weekly group and individual training sessions addressing relationship issues and communication skills to help students become successful decision makers as well as self-advocates. The counselor provides conflict resolution training to the students and works with the independent living assistants to help mediate conflict that arises between roommates.

Outcomes Matter

A recent survey conducted of LIFE graduates found that 96 percent of graduates had at least one paid employment position after graduation, while the remaining students had enrolled in additional postsecondary education. Just as important, over half (55 percent) of all graduates were living independently, which is more than three times the national average (16 percent) for adults with I/DD.

The application process is provided on our website. The eligibility criteria are that the student must have an intellectual disability. Our niche is that we provide the most supports available for a postsecondary program.

The ClemsonLIFE web site is :
    https://www.clemson.edu/education/programs/programs/culife/index.html

Dr. Joe Ryan, ClemsonLIFE, Sue Stanzione Distinguished Professorship

Chapter 10
Work

Work is an integral part of a self-advocate's life plan. **It's not typically about the money itself, but about nearly everything else.** Work helps develop skills, keeps their brains growing, provides a new environment to observe and engage with other people, and most importantly builds immense pride.

I remember when Gwendolyn got her job at Firehouse Subs sandwich shop. Her wide face could hardly contain her smile. She prepped food, boxed up cookies, cleaned the dining area, and occasionally interacted with customers. Gwendolyn learned how to follow instructions and how to voice her opinions or concerns. She learned about the importance of being on time and dressing appropriately. She saw how she was making a difference and always looked forward to her day at work. Gwendolyn worked one to three hours per day, two or three days a week. It was never going to make her rich, but it pushed her to focus and be responsible while making pocket change—*her* money.

Recall the financial discussion of chapter 8 and the decision families should proactively make: will my self-advocate be able to fund their own expenses primarily through work or through public benefits? We all wish for self-subsistence, but you must review the prospects and feasibility of securing a long-term, full-time job to provide the necessary income. Gwendolyn loves working, yet ten to fifteen hours per week is likely the most she can endure. She will need SSI, Medicaid, Social Security Retirement/ Survivorship/Disability (RSDI) benefits and more during her life. Thus, we consciously plan and coordinate those benefits with a level of work that provides her with spending money, confidence, and camaraderie without jeopardizing her public assistance. Your decision may be different, but as covered in chapter 8, **it is essential that each family consciously consider options and risks before starting employment.**

For all those who wish to work, whether a few hours a week or a full forty, the marketplace does need your self-advocate. It needs their skills, energy, and passion. That said, according to the Autism Housing Network, six years after high school, "55 percent of autistic individuals have no employment."[68] Statistics for the Down syndrome community are likely no better. The I/DD community is not looking for a handout, but to fill important roles in the diverse workforce of today. Approach the job search process with your head held high and seek the right match with your self-advocate.

Finding the Right Job

What type of job should your self-advocate consider? Sit down and talk about what kind of tasks your self-advocate enjoys, as you would with anyone looking for work. Do they like computer work, working with their hands, being inside or outside? Do they enjoy working with children or animals, cleaning, or office work like filing, mailings, or organizing? Do they enjoy art, music, or reading? When you identify tasks of interest, then their energy level will remain high.

Nearly every worksite could provide the right place—offices, day cares, hospitality industry, libraries, pet stores. While that first job may not be a career, it is their first opportunity to secure and hold a job. They will discover what they enjoy and dislike, and they will grow into other roles down the road.

For most of us, our favorite job was one that provided the right mix—applying our talents and interests in a welcoming and supportive work environment. Your self-advocate has the same goals. Seek a positive work environment, most especially the people your self-advocate will work with and their boss. Your family comes across a wide variety of responses to disabilities every day. Some people are scared, others may be frustrated by the need to repeat themselves or adjust to a slower pace, while others are warm and engaging from the beginning. They see through the stereotypes to the genuine warmth, kindness, and determination of our children. These are the people you want to employ your loved one because they care. They won't necessarily cut your self-advocate any slack, but they will spend the extra time to train them, check in on them, and help them grow.

Government-Assisted Job Searching

You might ask, "How do I find such a job for my self-advocate?" There are many federal, state, and local agencies poised to help apply for, secure, and maintain employment. When your self-advocate is in high school, include employment in your IEP discussions. Your school may help find jobs either within the school or the community and aid in transition and job coaching. They should also provide you with local governmental resources as part of their transition services.

You will find information through the US Department of Education's Vocational Rehabilitation agency and the Office of Disability Employment Policy (ODEP), though many of those resources focus on policy and employers more than self-advocates. The best place to start is through your state's workforce commission (see resources for link). Most cities have local offices that can offer assistance. They will meet with your self-advocate and talk about interests, help knock on doors, and even assist in training and monitoring going forward. In theory, this is a great help. However, in my experience, the level of assistance may be inconsistent and noncommittal. The case manager likely has dozens of cases and, even when motivated, is not able to dedicate the time necessary to find and maintain the right fit. Granted, every community is different, so do try working through those agencies to start. If they appear to provide valuable and timely assistance to secure the right fit, that can open up a world of opportunities and support. However, don't be surprised if this drawn-out process bears no fruit.

Parent-Directed Job Searching

If your self-advocate is in a day program or living in a residential community, these are natural places to start your search. Many offer job opportunities that may be of interest while providing a convenient location during the day. Every program needs office workers, cleaners, and assistants, while some also offer products (candles, flowers, artwork) and services (coffee houses, copying and mailing) to the public. Research these opportunities as part of your day program and residential living evaluations.

Otherwise, the best path is two-fold: your own network and your local stores. Sit down and consider the network of people your family knows—friends, teachers, doctors, members of your religious community. Do any of them own a business or work in a store that might need some assistance? Remember, **you are not asking for a handout but offering a cheerful, hardworking**

resource to do necessary tasks. This is how Gwendolyn secured her first job. The other path is to be prepared to go door-to-door at your nearby retail shopping areas. This is how Gwendolyn landed her second job. Be aware that your self-advocate will need proper identification. In lieu of a driver's license, you may need to present a state-issued identification card or passport.

Gwendolyn first job was with a parent of an adult with Down syndrome who owned an Edible Arrangements franchise. Gwendolyn's boss clearly understood how to care for and challenge her at work. Gwendolyn learned the ropes and took great pride in lancing cantaloupe onto skewers and cleaning up the kitchen.

When the shop suddenly closed, Gwendolyn and I worked together to find another job closer to home. Together, we made a résumé printed on fancy card stock. We practiced introductions and some interview questions. With documents in hand, we hit the road, knocking on retail doors near our house and leaving résumés. We tried a familiar pottery-making store, an office supply store, and even a recording studio, given her love for music. Finally, we approached Firehouse Subs. The line manager was welcoming and offered to share Gwendolyn's résumé with her manager, promising someone would call back. Sure enough, the manager called the next day, and we scheduled an in-store interview. I went with Gwendolyn to the interview. Once we arrived, I could see how caring the owner was in asking Gwendolyn questions and patiently listening for her answers. As they sat at a table for the formal interview, both the owner and Gwendolyn redirected me to the other end of the store. I observed from afar as Gwendolyn answered questions and shared her true personality. I was indeed a proud papa. Gwendolyn secured a job that day, but more importantly, she made a friend. Gwendolyn did her own scheduling with the owner and she made sure she arrived on time and worked hard. I huddled with the owner periodically, as we both wanted to ensure Gwendolyn was sufficiently challenged with new tasks. Over the years, they celebrated birthdays together, adapted through the pandemic together, and became friends and confidantes.

This arrangement was heaven-sent. It just dropped in our laps. Not all employment situations are that perfect. Be on guard for managers or coworkers who have less patience or may even become verbally abusive when they are under pressure. Pop in unannounced at times and ask your self-advocate how work and the relationships are going. The right arrangement is worth so much in their own independent development.

Other Work Options

Besides the customary work options above, your self-advocate may gain skills, camaraderie, and confidence through volunteer work at food pantries, charity shops, schools, or libraries. Any of these may evolve into paying jobs, or perhaps they are the perfect fit for your self-advocate as it stands.

You may also consider starting up a business of your own. Countless self-advocates are making art, clothing, books, food items, and more through their own businesses. It's a great way to learn, stretch, grow, and save while working within the support of family or friends. You can find many examples and role models on the NDSC and NDSS websites (specific links on our resources page).

On-the-Job Training

Training resources range from the typical provided by the manager or coworkers to coaches hired by some of the government agencies noted above or even the parent, depending on the work establishment. Encourage trainers to break down the tasks and provide laminated visual supports and checklists. The coach can assess if there is a need for assistive communication devices and training as well. They may also help the other staff to understand and appreciate how to engage with your self-advocate. This groundwork can lay a strong foundation and help change some of society's existing paradigms.

Ideally, the manager will provide a buddy as a resource, not just during initial orientation but for ongoing assistance and questions. Periodically check in with management for an update of how your self-advocate is doing—what needs more work and when additional tasks may be warranted. Monitor professionalism, including coming to work on time, wearing proper attire, turning off cell phones, and following instructions. Everyone needs assistance when starting a new job. The training and feedback will build further skills and confidence.

Money Management

Gwendolyn has always been proud of her work. She tells everyone about her job and what she does. She loves to save her money and occasionally spend it on something special. This has provided another learning opportunity—money management.

Before Gwendolyn began working, she had no concept for what things cost or the difference between $10, $100, or $1,000. Her job provided us the opportunity to talk about money. Gwendolyn has learned to use her smart phone calculator to add up her purchases as she shops and to calculate change when she pays cash. She will never invest her own money or pay her own bills, but she is developing a general appreciation.

We've gone to the grocery with a short shopping list and a $20 budget for her to manage. We shop together or she does the shopping and checkout alone while I wait at the front of the store. She is developing skills and pride in being able to do things others do. Eventually, we got Gwendolyn her own debit card. She carries it in her wallet and knows the PIN to complete transactions. We've talked about the sanctity of her debit card and PIN and even have others test her by asking for her PIN to reinforce the importance of privacy. She has a checking account to draw from which intentionally has a modest balance in case Gwendolyn gets carried away. Remember the asset limits from chapter 8 (generally $2,000), which include bank balances and credit card limits. Debit cards themselves are not an issue as they draw from their checking account.

Transportation Options

Securing a job or admittance into a day program prompts the question of transportation. It might seem like you've been driving carpool for decades because you probably have. But that is not necessarily a long-term solution, and transportation can play an important role in the Independence Plan. Depending on the size of your hometown, there may be several transportation options that provide a perfect growth plan for your self-advocate.

Specialized Public Transportation

Many cities offer public transportation specifically for those with disabilities. This is usually either a taxi or small van service that you schedule a day or more in advance. They come to your home and drop your self-advocate off at a designated location, e.g., school or work or shopping. Fares are usually subsidized by the city and thus quite reasonable. I consider these options safe but not always dependable. They may pick up several people and drop them off at a variety of locations, so the schedule is just an estimate. However, if your self-advocate has a flexible schedule, this is a great way for them to spread their wings and for you to be relieved of taxi duty. Make sure your self-advocate has a phone and you have them connected to your "Find a Friend" or similar app so that you know where they are at all times and are available for calls in case of emergency.

App-Based Transportation

Alternatives like taxis or app-based services such as Uber and Lyft are also options. You can schedule any of these via phone app or teach your self-advocate how to do this with the aid of a handy checklist. Since payment happens on the app, it requires no debit/credit card or cash and is door-to-door service. The cost may be prohibitive for daily service, but these options can be handy when you need them.

Public Transportation

Public transportation is the most independent option to consider, especially if the commute is short and direct. You can teach your self-advocate where to go, at what time to catch a specific bus, and where to get off. This option also depends on how far they must walk to get to and from the bus. It sounds scary just thinking about it, but with practice, public transportation is feasible. I suggest starting with simple routes to rehearse the logistics and communication with the bus driver and other patrons before contemplating lengthier, more complex routes. In either case you may choose to follow the bus the first couple of days to ensure your self-advocate does get off the bus at the right stop.

Gwendolyn's first job and her post–high school education program at Friends of Down Syndrome were quite a distance from home. We used the specialized public transportation program for her commute. As noted above, it was far from perfect regarding timing, but we never had any security or safety issues, and Gwendolyn was quite proud of managing her commute on her own. Her subsequent job with Firehouse Subs was just a couple of blocks from our home.

<u>Walking Independently</u>

Gwendolyn and I walked the two blocks together to and from work for the first couple of weeks until she said she was ready to walk by herself. We took a couple of more trips together, noting the hazards along the way including curbs, the absence of sidewalks on one side of the street, and crossing the one intersection. We practiced looking both ways and she built her confidence. After I walked her to work one day, I asked if she was ready to walk home by herself. Her face lit up and she said yes. A couple of hours later I waited for her as she popped around the corner from work and safely navigated the intersection. About three quarters of the way across, she started to gallop, leaping into my arms on the sidewalk. She was so happy and repeated "I did it all by myself!" several times. What a memorable moment for the two of us and even more importantly, a significant building block for her growth and confidence.

Job searches and work programs, money management, and transportation are all huge steps in your self-advocate's Independence Plan. They may seem out of reach at times, but by building their independent mindset and confidence through tasks at home, these too are not only possible but essential parts of their journey to become an independent adult.

Jonathan shares an inspiring story of his son, Fionn's, insatiable curiosity and drive to see—and impact—the world.

Family Feature
Fionn's Story

We are Jonathan, Veronica, and Fionn. We currently live in Ireland. Fionn is twenty-six and has Down syndrome.

Years ago, we asked our teenage son, Fionn, what he wanted to do when he grows up. He said he wanted to be the next David Attenborough (BBC nature presenter). A week later, we asked him again. He said a professional violinist. The next time, a director of scifi/fantasy films. Then a member of One Direction.

Such ambition, and what a great opportunity for a research project. If we explored each possibility in turn (but maybe not the world-famous boy band one, directly), not only would he then be able to make a more informed choice, but we could share the process with other families, to inform and inspire their own searching.

We set up a social enterprise, with Fionn and Jonathan as its first (and only) employees, called Fionnathan Productions. Financial help came from two government grants amounting to a quarter-time contract for each of us. Veronica is our company secretary on the board of directors. We have probably two of the most extensive job descriptions on the planet. Fionn's includes:

Searching for Structure

Fionn's first task was a very practical one: searching for his own apartment. It's certainly work, so why not be paid for it? He scoured notices online, arranged viewing of suitable apartments, researched and applied for any government help he was entitled to, and eventually, signed a lease on his first apartment. Soon after, he did the same for an art studio.

Redistributing Food

What's the best thing to do with perfectly good food that is about to be destroyed when supermarkets clear shelf space for new stuff? From our point of view, the best thing to do is to eat it. So, to disrupt the food waste chain (and get free food!) we partnered with a much larger social enterprise who brokered deals with three local shops. But we quickly realized the donations were ten times what we could eat ourselves. So Fionn started knocking on doors all around his neighborhood, dragging his wagon around and making new friends. We now have a network of two dozen families who share the food we get. Fionn has developed a lot of social capital through this good deed.

The Search for Happiness Project

As already mentioned, Fionn has a long list of life goals. To help him narrow his career aims, he interviews people who are successful in his fields of interest, asking celebrities and regular citizens, "What do you love about your life?" Our YouTube channel, "Fionnathan Presents: What Do You Love?" has over 600 of these interviews with more than three million views!

Guest Lectures

It seems to us that most adults with Down syndrome have less choice and control in their lives than other adults do, though clearly that's not true in Fionn's case. We want to share our innovative approach with the people who will be in position to bring systematic changes, so we reached out to various programs at many universities. Students and their professors find our talks fresh and stimulating. We have given over fifty such talks at over thirty institutions. College students often say, "Fionn, I'm envious of your life."

And that is just a taste of what Fionn's job entails. He often plays his fiddle on the streets of Galway and elsewhere, has done work on multiple film projects, works in politics and policy as a community advocate, and seeks amazing nature experiences from the Amazon to Zanzibar, which he has shared with over 10,000 school children.

And we're just getting started. (Or not, because we've always said the day Fionn decides he no longer wants to be a social entrepreneur is the day we wrap up Fionnathan.) Next, Fionn wants to move our base of operations to America. See you soon.

Anything's possible. Or maybe everything's possible—we'll let you know.

Jonathan, Fionn's dad

Chapter 11
Community Inclusion

To be honest, "inclusion" was always a sensitive word for us. Sure, as new parents of a beautiful daughter with Down syndrome, we had ambitious dreams for Gwendolyn. We wanted her to be happy and do as much as possible. We wanted her to be a contributing part of the community around her...to be included!

School Inclusion: For Better or for Worse

Parenting a child with disabilities through the school system is not an easy task. Most parents recognize this early on when ARDs and IEPs become common vernacular. Parents are often driven toward inclusion and prompted to fight the school system at every opportunity.

I remember when Gwendolyn was around six and ready to go to kindergarten. The buzz around our local Down syndrome association (DSA) was "inclusion at all costs." We should be prepared to fight to have our daughter in all mainstream academic classes with the necessary tools and assistance. Anything short of that would be detrimental to Gwendolyn's development and a failure as parents. What a heavy weight to bear!

Nevertheless, we prepared our points, consulted with others at our DSA, and went to battle at Gwendolyn's first ARD meeting. I'm sure the administrators and teachers saw us coming as we fumbled through notes and words to plead our case. Somewhat surprisingly, we succeeded in getting her into the mainstream kindergarten class. The rest of the meeting was less tense as we populated her IEP plan with step-by-step goals. We walked away from the meeting proud of our accomplishments and optimistic for Gwendolyn's development.

Course Correction

However, reality set in a couple of months later. Gwendolyn was spending about half her day in the special needs classes to address her life skills goals and then a buddy would walk her to the mainstream class three times a day for a dose of inclusion. We had visited that classroom several times and observed Gwendolyn off to the side, coloring or playing with puzzle pieces by herself as more academic concepts were presented to the other students. We shared our frustration with the teacher who remarked that they had tried to involve her but to no avail. We challenged the earnestness of their attempts and encouraged the administrators to work their magic, yet further feedback and visits were not fruitful.

My wife and I chose to step back and ponder the situation. What were our goals and expectations for Gwendolyn? This can be a humbling question. No one wants to give up or establish perceived limitations for any of their children. We've learned never to underestimate her drive or abilities, but a dose of realism can be healthy as well. Our hope for Gwendolyn was that she would talk, read, and write, develop relationships and form caring and loving bonds, actively engage in pleasing hobbies, and have the ability to work. We hadn't yet thought about independent living but that would be added to the list later.

With this in mind, we felt it was most important for Gwendolyn to learn these skills starting in kindergarten. We considered holding firm and fighting, insisting on a teacher's assistant, and more classroom inclusion. However, we remained skeptical that could happen, especially considering the teacher was neither trained nor inclined to provide that for Gwendolyn. More importantly, we realized that was not the class to address most of our priorities. Furthermore, the environment was far from inclusive with Gwendolyn secluded to the side. Even with life skills classes, she could still benefit from inclusion in school activities, hobbies, playgroups, and with her siblings at home.

What Is Best for Your Family?

I would counsel you to take advice but filter it through your own family situation. What is truly best for your child with Down syndrome? Perhaps they are prepared for full inclusion, and you can secure a teacher's assistant to make that a reality. Perhaps they will benefit most from a more purposeful curriculum taught by teachers accustomed to developing children with disabilities.

This is a tough decision that we revisited with Gwendolyn most years. Ultimately, we decided to remove Gwendolyn from the mainstream kindergarten class and focus our energies on her critical life and social skills at her pace. Over the years, she developed personal hygiene skills, she is a solid reader, her writing and penmanship are excellent, and her communication and relationship skills are good and evolving.

She has benefited from her younger sibling role models tremendously, as well as her exposure to gymnastics, horseback riding, swimming, biking, and world travel. She loves her music and is quite comfortable surfing the internet to research her favorite artists. She is an ardent calendar follower which helps her maintain her routines and prepare for those exceptions that lie ahead. She has worked part-time and loves the camaraderie and pride of accomplishment. She rides her bike alone and with friends and she advocates for herself and her personal independence. I'd say Gwendolyn has done a pretty awesome job!

However, there are many other examples of quite successful full inclusion education. **Consider family goals, advocate where you truly believe it is important and will make a positive difference and strive to create growth opportunities for your loved one through school, hobbies, and at home.** These school-aged years, after all, present the building blocks for lifelong independence and, ironically, community inclusion. Examine your alternatives. Talk to the school but also to parents and advocates that can help you weigh options and pursue the program best for your loved one.

Community-at-Large

Many families have staunch views of community inclusion. Brooke's mom, Ramona Hebert, says, "I want my daughter not to just be a taker but also a giver" within the broader community. Where will your adult with Down syndrome live and work? Will they be in a day program only for those with intellectual and developmental disabilities (I/DD)? Will they live at home or in a specialized residential living community, or within the community-at-large? How will they integrate with the general public? How can they learn and make a difference with others?

These are all important questions to consider with your own self-advocate. What do they want? What will promote their personal growth, positive relationships, pride, and confidence?

Through such probing conversations, **you may identify which are their true priorities and which may be your own dreams that you are compelled to impose upon them.** For Gwendolyn, she treasures the relationships with her peers that have I/DD, but she also loves to converse with others. She now lives in a residential living community with hundreds of other adults with various disabilities. She has worked in food prep with the opportunity to converse with coworkers and the public. Gwendolyn also loves to spend time with family at home and through travels, sharing her accomplishments with grandparents, aunts, and uncles and fielding questions from cousins. We all believe we have struck the right balance for Gwendolyn.

Whether you opt to assume the homeschooling teacher's role or enroll your loved one in a day program, find employment, or enter a college program, continue to guide them to discover the community and world around them. They will build self-confidence and their dreams and ambitions will continue to evolve.

Gwendolyn continues to practice her community skills by ordering her own meals, advocating for herself, and interfacing with others while being cognizant of the Social Circles Model presented in chapter 4 and the safety and security measures described in chapter 6. Your family's goals and the right balance for your loved one may be different from ours. How can you help make *their* ambitions come true?

The Down Syndrome Community

I never really paid much attention to the broad range of abilities and challenges within the Down syndrome community before I began work on The UPLifting Guidebook Project. This project has given me the great fortune to meet amazing families around the world. I've gotten to hear their stories, struggles, and successes. I've realized the Down syndrome community is indeed a broad spectrum of abilities and dreams.

Even within our own community, we are often disconnected and far from inclusive, despite our global need for sharing, learning, supporting, and advocating together. Through my discussions, I've met families that feel they are excluded from most social events, learning topics, or resource funding through local or national Down syndrome organizations because their self-advocate is nonverbal, overweight, "lower-functioning," or indeed "higher functioning," or dual diagnosis with autism. Yes, these labels make us different or exceptional, and as a community we should fight to celebrate our uniqueness and clamor for community inclusion. **We also need to "start at home" and respect the various challenges within our community.** How can we support and learn from each other? After all, don't we all have our distinct challenges...and strengths and beauty?

In chapter 7, I described the prevalence of autism within our Down syndrome community. These families met the challenge of an at- or near-birth diagnosis of Down syndrome and all the heartache and joy that comes along with that, only to notice other physical or behavioral traits often masked by the vagaries of Down syndrome but later diagnosed as autism. I think we can all envision how overwhelming that could be! Yet nearly every family I met with a dual diagnosis indicated they felt alone. They no longer felt welcomed into the Down syndrome community given the behavioral differences, nor into the autism community given their obvious physical traits. And the families also recognized that their issues were not additive—Down syndrome *plus* autism challenges—but in some ways exponential because the combination presented unique physical and mental health obstacles which could make accomplishing seemingly routine tasks nearly impossible. Ethan's mother, Rosaura, implores that she needs community to share issues and solutions, as well as social time together. Yet she and Ethan often feel ignored. You can hear more about their frustrations and progress in this chapter's **Family Feature**.

What do these families need during such moments of crisis? Understanding, ideas, support, and helpful resources from our community—from us.

Let us all use this as an opportunity to be inclusive first within the broad definition of our Down syndrome community, and then within the broader society so that our own self-advocates can achieve the goals and dreams that they themselves establish.

Rosaura shares their heartbreaking story of her family and her son Ethan's strength. As she states, they "belong to two different villages, the Down syndrome village and the autistic one. One foot on each side, never fully on either."

Family Feature
Ethan's Story

When Ethan was discharged from the hospital, they sent us to meet with the social worker. I don't remember much of our conversation, but I do remember saying I was looking forward to watching him reach his milestones.

I anticipated enjoying being a mom and loving this baby and teaching him and learning from him. I wanted to see and celebrate the first time he held his head while on his tummy, the first time he rolled over, and so on. I didn't know what to expect but I knew his development would be different. I just didn't know in what way. The social worker reassured me that all those milestones would come, but just at a slower pace.

Very few things Ethan has accomplished in his life have come easy to him. Holding his head, rolling over, walking...oh God, walking. He wanted so much to walk, and I spent weeks and months encouraging him to creep as much as possible because I had read it would help his brain and his ability to walk. He persisted every step of the way and slowly he mastered those prized milestones.

However, some behaviors that I began to observe concerned me. Ethan couldn't tolerate getting his nails cut. His cries and screams would make you think I was inflicting some serious pain on him. Also, he couldn't tolerate any texture in his food. It had to be velvety smooth, or he couldn't eat it. He would also shake his hands in front of his eyes or would tune out from reality as if seeing things I couldn't see.

There was also the head shaking from side to side while balancing on his tummy. He enjoyed doing that. Leaving him for a couple of hours in a small day care a friend ran out of her home was terribly stressful to him. Loud noises and kids running around was too much for him. I'd find him with quiet tears rolling down his face, seeking refuge on a sofa. Of course, the experiment lasted only a couple of days. After going through pre-k, we decided to homeschool. Still, I tried homeschooling classes, after-school programs, and other ways to keep him with his peers and hopefully have some social time and some free time for myself. They just didn't work.

Ethan was officially diagnosed as autistic at age seven. The diagnosis was mild to moderate autism. I left crying and couldn't stop all the way home. Why? Why was he being robbed of his childhood?

I've learned not to share Ethan's diagnosis of autism, if at all possible. I've just decided to let people draw their own conclusions if they wish. Having a child with two life-changing diagnoses seems to bring both the best and the worst of people, even people in the special needs community.

The issue with having a dual diagnosis is that you don't seem to fit in anywhere. The kids with only Down syndrome appear to do so much physically and are often sassy and in constant motion. The kids with only autism usually are a lot taller than my son, often very proficient in speech, and have strong interests. I'm a stranger in two worlds that I have been assigned but don't fully understand.

Through the years I've continued with my efforts to find our tribe. I've joined other moms at the playground but while the other kids were having a great time with the sprinkler and the playground equipment, I would always end up walking after Ethan because he wanted to get away from the screaming and running, so we'd go exploring instead. I started taking him to the playground by myself when there was hardly anyone around. He loved it then.

While there are kind, evolved individuals who see in Ethan's beautiful soul a boy who wants to connect and have fun, there are many others that see him with fear in their hearts; a fear that reveals itself on the stares and expressions on their faces when he's engaging in echolalia, or repetition of noises or phrases. I try to be understanding because I know it's a fear of their own frailty that they are forced to confront by the sight of a boy who looks, behaves, and acts differently. On days when I'm discouraged, I just don't feel so understanding and despise those faces.

I've made attempts, again and again, to find friends for my son but we belong to two different villages, the Down syndrome village and the autistic one. One foot on each side, never fully on either. The hardest part has been to witness the reactions of people who, one would think, would be understanding—those dealing with their own special needs child within their family. As an example, once I got in touch with a mom whose child with autism seemed to have similar interests to mine. We started planning a playdate for the boys and for us moms to meet. As soon as I mentioned that my son also had a diagnosis of Down syndrome, the excuses started, and that was the end of that.

Another time, a mom whose son has Down syndrome about the same age as Ethan was looking for friends for her son. As soon as I told her about Ethan also having autism she disappeared from our lives before we even met.

To be fair, we have found a couple of times where the moms agreed to see if a friendship could blossom with our kids but Ethan's inability to converse and delay in producing a response to a question hasn't been the recipe for another child to persist but still, I'm grateful for the opportunity.

I completely understand the natural instinct to protect one's children, but Ethan is and has always been no threat to himself or others. He longs to connect and make people laugh. He's very good at reading people and knows when someone needs a smile and a hug. He hugs you because he has grown to love you or because he knows you could use a hug.

Practically all Down syndrome events are geared toward the "typical" Down syndrome population. I'm fortunate that Ethan can still participate in most of them to an extent. It also helps that most volunteers helping in various programs are willing to adjust to accommodate his sensory defensiveness. I go to as many events as I can where I know Ethan is going to enjoy himself, always hoping he'll connect with others.

Every year our local Down syndrome association does fundraising, gathering impressive sums of money but no programs are ever offered for the dual diagnosis population.

I watch the kids that only have the Down syndrome diagnosis and I cry inside. I know I always will but I'm thankful it's more my issue than Ethan's. Ethan is aware of being different, no matter what village we are visiting: the autistic village, the Down syndrome village, or the neurotypical village where invariably, kids of all ages stare at him. He takes it in stride. I see him in deep thought, processing his environment, and making the decision to make the best of it.

Would I remove the diagnosis from his body and brain if I had the power? Absolutely! He would still be my wonderful Ethan but without the limitations to his abilities or his chances to connect with others. Regardless, I feel honored to be called his mom.

Rosaura, Ethan's mom

SECTION IV — TAKING ON THE WORLD

SECTION V
HOME IS WHERE THE HEART IS

Our UPL Family Survey indicates most advocates and families want independence—the ability to make choices and live with personal freedom without reliance on others. There is no independence topic more delicate than where your self-advocate should live.

When Gwendolyn was born our expectations shifted. Suddenly, we expected she would live with us the rest of our lives and move in with one of her siblings thereafter. We heard the phrase "forever child" and felt that was Gwendolyn's future and ours was the forever caregiver. As we experienced her slower development, and our greater hands-on involvement in her toddler years, as well as her greater fragility and vulnerability in those early years, our premonition seemed to be confirmed. The first thoughts of her moving out of our house were met with doubt, fear, and shame. We felt such a move would not be in her best interest and we would be shirking our parental duties. However, through more research and discussions, we became familiar with the wide variety of options available, as well as Gwendolyn's own desire for independence, including living on her own. Our overwhelming emotions began to transition from fear and guilt to excitement and pride. Such a change was *not* evading our duty but was, as with her siblings, providing her with an amazing opportunity to flourish beyond the safe umbrella of parents and home. We now reject classifying Gwendolyn as the "forever child." She is a successful young adult with many more opportunities in front of her. We just needed to find the right home that would align with her specific abilities and interests.

We have considered Gwendolyn's skills and desires and made a choice for our family. Your choice may be different now and perhaps change later. In either case, this section will help you prepare for the option(s) you may choose. Chapter 12 presents a broad array of choices, from living with family to provider- and consumer-directed housing. Subsequent chapters discuss amenities and considerations for any home option, followed by specific steps for finding a new home if/when you are ready.

Section V: Plans and Actions		
#	Action	Life Stage*
1	Consider drivers for family-based housing	Early Adulthood
2	Consider community-based housing options	Early Adulthood
3	Consider Core Priorities and Life Enhancement amenities	Early Adulthood
4	Develop list of community-based housing options	Early Adulthood
5	Download the Housing Evaluation Template and populate	Early Adulthood

If your loved one has passed this stage but has not completed this action, place this at the top of your action plan

Check out resources and references at the back of the book. Downloads are available for free at:

http://www.beyonddownsyndrome.net/The-Essential-Guide

Chapter 12
Housing Options:
From Family- to Community-Based

High school is over, and most parents assume their loved one will continue to live in the family home. In fact, our UPL Family Survey indicates that when it comes to living outside the home, 45 percent have "not even really thought about it."[69] Many people prefer to put off this difficult issue until life forces decisions. However, that is a choice fraught with future risks. Consider your options early so you can prepare everyone's mindset, as well as your budget and benefits.

Living in a Family Home

Since your self-advocate is already living at the family home, let's examine common drivers for your loved one to remain there:

1. **This has always been the expectation**: Most parents assume their loved one will live at home, if they think about it at all. However, options have broadened and dramatically improved over the last few decades, and it is important to understand the responsibilities of being a caregiver of an adult.

2. **Companionship for the parent**: Especially as one gets older, the bond provides warmth and familiarity. There may also be a level of dependency as the child in many ways becomes the caregiver.

3. **Financial benefits of taking care of someone with I/DD at home**: If the self-advocate is receiving state Medicaid social services such as home/community–based (HCS) benefits, the parent could be designated as a caregiver and compensated by the state for providing services for their child such as occupational therapy and day program–type activities. According to Barbara Bush,[70] applying for this classification through your state's Medicaid Services System is rather simple. However, some states have decades-long waitlists, the compensation varies, and the number of hours awarded is determined by your state's Medicaid waiver program. The obligations are plentiful, including documentation of services and maintaining purposeful programming.

4. **Fear that their vulnerable child will not be safe and secure**: Parents are naturally protective of all their family. Unique physical limitations or communication and advocacy skills may place your loved one at greater risk within the general public. As we discussed in chapter 6: Safety & Security, there are precautions and adaptations for mitigating these risks. While some housing options may not be able to support certain challenges, others specialize in providing such accommodations.

5. **Confidence that the parent knows best and will provide/ advocate better than others**: While it is true that the parents know their loved one best, they may be less capable

to address these needs. Caregivers should stay abreast of current technologies and learning approaches, as well as maintain a wide variety of activities to push through inevitable plateaus and avoid regression syndrome.

6. **Feeling of shame or dereliction of duty in moving your child out**: As covered in the first section on mindset, this is a difficult sentiment to overcome if you have always expected to be the lifelong caregiver. However, here are two vital considerations that may bring you comfort. First, always strive to maintain a person-centered approach. What is best for your loved one? What will support their continued growth and development and provide them with self-confidence and pride? The other reflection is that you, the parent, do not have to discard your own long-term plans just because your child has Down syndrome. Retirement and relaxation are legitimate aspirations that can be fulfilled and may actually help you be a happier person and a better parent. You are working hard to provide and advocate for your loved one. You deserve contentment. Guilt and shame have no place in your consideration.

If you feel that your loved one should continue to live with you long term, consider the above six drivers. Likely some of these apply to you, as they did to us. However, **the process of examining them helped to remove the heavy weight of guilt and expectations so we could evaluate options in terms of what is truly best for our loved one with Down syndrome.**

Adult Life at Home

What would living at home look like? Some of it could look the same as it has in the past. However, if your loved one has been in public school for the last twelve to sixteen years, once that ends their day opens up. They will need to be engaged to keep learning and contributing. You may evaluate local day programs and seek out work options in the area as described in section III. Otherwise, their continued development will rest squarely on your shoulders.

Just having your self-advocate join your errands and appointments is not enough. You will initiate their activities and this will become your priority. You will, in essence, become their homeschooling teacher with field trips to broaden the mind and playgroups to sharpen their communications and social skills. This could include trips to the library or museums, group socials, volunteering, or taking community courses together. Consider what this could look like and your ability and interest in fulfilling that role. Daniel's mom, Carolyn, enjoys the camaraderie and considers her son a roommate, yet she also admits sometimes she "feels like a glorified Uber driver."

Amanda's mom, Joyce, exclaims, "Every individual and circumstance is different. Retiring and caring for my daughter hasn't been exhausting. It has been quite the opposite. It has allowed me to do all the things I've been wanting to do with [Amanda] that I couldn't while working as a single parent. I feel like I am playing catch up, quite frankly. We are having a great time together because she can better communicate her needs and continues to learn new things every day."

Consider Living at Home as Temporary

However, you must be prepared for the future. Perhaps your self-advocate's skill may begin to regress and the need for greater care and exposure can become immediate. Maybe you, the caregiver, are no longer able to care for your loved one because they become too much for you to handle, you become incapacitated, or you pass away. Let's face it, at least one of these situations will happen at some point.

According to *A Place in the World,*[71] 5.4 million individuals with intellectual/developmental disabilities live in the home of a family caregiver. Of those, 25 percent or 1.3 million individuals live with a caregiver over the age of sixty. **Given that people with Down syndrome are living considerably longer than before, many now outlive their caregivers. Now more than ever, it is important to consider options and have a long-term caregiver plan.**

Our greatest fear has been that in such unpredictable circumstances, either an unprepared relative assumes custody or Gwendolyn becomes a ward of the state. We must ensure neither scenario occurs.

If you currently plan for your loved one to live at home, you should select one of the following long-term options:

- **Relativity:** Your loved one could eventually move in with a relative such as an aunt, uncle, or sibling. In this scenario, have extensive discussions with your relative. Do they understand the day-to-day caregiving and financial obligations? Could they move in the future, necessitating another reset of activities and public benefits? Do you foresee they can and will provide such support for the remainder of your loved one's life, or will other options need to be set up later? How will your self-advocate adjust to such a transition?

- **Transitions:** Transitional programs are relatively new choices in the I/DD market, helping self-advocates to learn additional independent skills and practice living either within residential communities or in their own house or apartment. These private-pay arrangements are intentionally short term (typically three to five years) to provide that bridge to community-based living.[72] You could also consider more conventional transitions such as an in-law suite or an above-garage apartment on your property. You will then need to consider sustainable community-based housing given the temporary nature of this choice.

- **Community-based home:** Research and plan for a move to a community-based home at a later date. The second half of this chapter will cover the many options in this category.

Whether you are prepared for one of these options now or shelve it for later, you can't just note this in your Independence Plan and leave it. Do some research into these options. Have discussions within your family, with impacted relatives, and with transitional or community-based residential living options. Budget for your preference and include it in your letter of intent. Given that your preferences may have waiting lists, create a short-term solution with relatives if you choose not to enroll your loved one in transitional or long-term housing solutions now.

Often, change happens abruptly when family conditions shift. You may not have the chance to make the necessary arrangements at that time. Consider the impact of an abrupt change for your self-advocate, especially if it is prompted by a family member's health problems or death. Be sure you and others provide comfort and support to your self-advocate during such trying times.

Regardless of your timeline for longer term housing, our UPL Family Survey[73] found the most common obstacles to moving out of the family home were as follows (respondents could choose more than one option):

- Self-advocate readiness (28 percent)
- Financial resources (35 percent)
- Overly protective parents (41 percent)
- Lack of understanding of options or availability of guidance on how to proceed (60 percent)

In other words, sometimes the self-advocate needs more independent skill sets and exposure and often the family has not aligned their mindsets or resources as part of a long-term plan. Interestingly, the Survey was completed by the parents, so the results underscore their acknowledged role and apprehensions.

Ready or Not?

Most self-advocates are searching for independence—the opportunity to do things for themselves and be a productive, inclusive part of their community. They want to be involved in the decisions affecting them, and their interests may surprise you. According to the Autism Housing Network, **"87 percent of autistic adults live with their parents but only 22 percent want to live there."**[74] While there are no such statistics for adults with Down syndrome, we can assume the situation is similar.

How do you know if your loved one is ready for such a move? Carolyn, mother of Daniel who is twenty-nine and lives at home, has collected these real-life leading indicators:

1. They look with envy at grown-up people in their life who have moved out, gone to college, or gotten married.
2. They exhibit increased frustration behavior such as talking back or arguing.
3. They refuse to go or don't want to go with the parents anymore.
4. They tell you, "Hey Mom, I want to move into a place of my own."
5. They use their communication device to tell you by pointing to an apartment or a house.
6. You find your young adult looking in magazines for ideas on home decorating.
7. They pack their room into boxes and refuse to take their stuff out.
8. You see them going to Zillow to check out houses.
9. They tell others they are looking for a roommate.
10. If you present scenarios, they pick one that shows them living in a place of their own.

What if your loved one is not ready for such a move? This is not a change you want to force on your self-advocate. It can be helpful to have discussions, for them to join some tours, and perhaps to practice by having camp sleepovers or weekends at a friend or relative's house. Eventually, with your encouragement, the possibilities will become intriguing.

When to Evaluate Your Long-Term Options

The time for change may be years down the road, but given the magnitude of this choice, this is not a decision to be taken lightly or with short notice. Carefully consider your criteria and options so that you can prepare your mindset, your budget, and your self-advocate's skill set.

Community-Based Housing Options

You may be surprised at the current breadth of community-based housing options with varying degrees of abilities and independence. *A Place in the World* indicates a national survey by The Arc found 87 percent of people with I/DD hope to live within the community at some point (including 62 percent in their own home or apartment, 14 percent supervised group home, 8 percent planned community or campus living).[75] Let's evaluate the plethora of options.

Provider- vs. Consumer-Directed Housing

The first broad stroke when evaluating community-based housing is to consider provider- and consumer-directed housing.

For provider-directed, someone else is in charge, generally the staff or an agency. They organize programming, meals, off-campus trips, admission and roommates, transportation, communications, and often work opportunities. The provider controls the agenda and so, in many ways, the choices for your self-advocate and the communication with your family. Indeed, this category may offer the widest array of activities for your loved one, as well as the most sustainable housing options. You and your loved one will depend on the staff to meet the various considerations covered in the next chapter, so closely observe and evaluate each option. Consumer-directed means that the consumer, your loved one, is in charge, likely with some assistance from yourself. Together, you will select the home. You will negotiate terms of the lease, any supportive services needed, separate day programs, meals, transportation, and a roommate if desired. Based on your unique individual, you will have to determine what tasks your self-advocate is responsible for and have the comfort that they will contact either contractors or yourself if they cannot manage a situation. This category suits those able to be more proactive. Your loved one may meet these criteria today or perhaps this may be a possible goal down the road, based on further growth and development within the provider-directed options.

It's important to remember **the objective is not to place your loved one into the most independent home possible, but to find the right fit for their skills and interests.** That will ensure the most successful and sustainable situation. Although this process can be tedious, your choice of their first home may not be the last. Based on your loved one's growth, their physical and mental health needs, and financial resources available, you may change specific homes or home categories several times. That said, this is not a decision to be taken lightly. These evaluations can take considerable time and emotional energy. Seek the right home for your loved one for now and for the foreseeable future. Then introduce some flexibility to adapt, if and when necessary.

Less Independent			More Independent		
Provider-Directed			**Consumer-Directed**		
Institutions	Group Homes	Assisted-Living Communities	Independent Communities	Sharing Homes	Personal Homes

Provider-Directed Housing
• Institutions

Despite many advancements in disability care, institutions are typically rather sterile state facilities, often psychiatric hospitals, charged with providing care for people with mental health issues. Traditionally, this was the home for most people with I/DD. However, times have changed. Parents, doctors, and society in general have recognized that no matter the abilities of the self-advocate, this is likely not the best home for anyone with Down syndrome. People with Down syndrome need compassion, patience, physical/occupational/speech therapy, and caring attention focused on developing skills and mindset. Residents here will have little say in their care and their days will likely be dictated by staff schedules in an effort to keep the peace, not necessarily serve the community. Since a wide range of people are serviced by these institutions, resources often go to the more extreme cases. While the staff at institutions may be quite skilled and well-intentioned, these facilities are not set up or prepared to provide the assistance our loved one requires.

While my intent here is not to recommend any one option but to lay them out for you to assess based on your family's needs and desires, these institutions rarely fit anyone's Independence Plan. However, in the case of the death or disability of the caregiver, if no other housing option is arranged or provided for, your self-advocate could become a ward of the state and placed into these institutions.

• Group Homes

Group homes are typically public programs in which an agency buys or rents a home and hires a caregiver to live in the home 24/7, providing support to four to six adults with disabilities living in that home. The caregiver can customize care to each resident based on abilities and interest, so some may do laundry and others may help with the cooking. Because they are funded by the state, typically these agencies must accept any nonviolent, same-sex individuals seeking to live in a group home. The agency cannot be selective, nor can the individuals or families. For example, they can't seek to maintain a Down syndrome–only home or one with similar interests, behaviors, or age groups. The families also can't select, manage, or fire the home caregiver, although agencies may accept and consider counsel. Some also have a day program or are affiliated with one. All residents are expected to either attend that day program or perhaps another in order to provide respite for the caregiver, who may also have another day job or attend classes. The agency and resident caregiver will also plan shopping or entertainment outings at night or especially on the weekend. Typically, all residents must attend the outings since no one can stay home alone. Some agencies may have several homes in the neighborhood and coordinate socials and trips within their housing network, in which case accommodations can be made for those preferring not to join a group activity. Group homes can meet the needs of self-advocates and their families, but the lack of control over decisions impacting the environment must be considered.

• Assisted-Living Community

Living communities are typically campuses with adults with various intellectual/developmental disabilities, often with co-located day programs and residential homes. Staff aim to provide structure that will help residents develop and grow their life skills, vocational skills, and social skills. Assisted-living communities serve those needing more assistance. Twenty-four/seven oversight is provided in the dorm or housing building and staff are there to support with schedule and medication reminders. Day programs can often be vibrant with many options. Security and safety should be paramount, and residents don't leave campus until checked out by their guardian or approved family member or for organized trips to town. If your loved one is fairly independent, enjoys activities and socializing with others, but needs some assistance or reminders through the day, these communities may be the perfect fit.

Consumer-Directed Housing
• Independent Living Community
These living communities are similar to the assisted-living communities described above. Often these more independent housing options are co-located with assisted-living options and provide progressive choices as residents continue to develop and grow their independence. Residents at independent communities may often live in their own apartment or suite on campus. The community may provide a plethora of day program activities, work options, and social venues. Residents can spread their wings by cooking their own meals, doing their own laundry and meds, and even driving or taking public transportation off-campus for work, shopping, or entertainment. Staff is available on campus but not in each living quarter. Other options may include a group of apartments with staff within the complex providing assistance, transportation, and activities. This option suits those individuals who have the skills and initiative to take care of themselves under most daily conditions.

• Sharing Homes
Sharing homes is a private version of group homes. In this instance, one or more individuals with disabilities share a house, condo, apartment, or townhome with at least one neurotypical individual who may be a relative or friend of the family, perhaps

a college student or senior citizen. People in this role receive companionship and serve a greater community purpose while perhaps receiving compensation or a discount on their portion of the rent in exchange for overseeing the others. This arrangement is often best suited for more independent individuals, but it really depends on the abilities, interest, and time availability of the neurotypical housemate. The home could be rented by any one of the residents or owned by one or more of the residents who charge rent to the others. Since this is a private venture, residents control roommate selection, and may themselves direct the "rules of the house" with some guidance from the families. Everyone is responsible for arranging their own day program, work, and other activities along with the necessary transportation. In some cases, the owner or tenant may be eligible for a Housing and Urban Development (HUD) housing choice voucher (HCV) in which the owner of the home pays only 30 percent of their monthly adjusted gross income for mortgage/rent plus utilities. This is a fully consumer-directed, independent option that benefits from oversight and community. Guardian involvement is likely necessary to monitor and amend arrangements, including contracts for the specific house, roommates, and caregiver.

• Personal Homes

The most independent option is an apartment, condo, townhome or other housing in which a person with disabilities resides. They could have roommates and the structure may look similar to the shared homes version, but without any on-premises support. This option should be considered for the most independent individuals.

It is important to note that while these six housing categories are arranged by perceived level of independence, you should evaluate each based on the criteria noted in the next chapter. You might expect some categories to be stronger on certain considerations, but there is a wide range of services, security, and quality within each group. Therefore, it is essential to research viable housing options. Ask probing questions, keenly observe during tours, and test with follow-up inquiries to assure yourselves of the amenities and the level of service they deliver. Chapter 14 presents the process for selecting the right home in any category.

You may wish to print out the Housing Evaluation Template, a handy grid of options and criteria, free on our website (www. beyonddownsyndrome.net/The-Essential-Guide) to prepare for your search and to narrow your options in a methodical fashion.

The Independent Housing Market

As adults with Down syndrome live longer and the wave of independence for people with I/DD sweeps through families and society in general, families have a growing number of options. However, this is a market in short supply, with demand expected to grow exponentially. Desiree Kameka Galloway, director of the Autism Housing Network, insists "the biggest challenge is availability."[76] With long waitlists, start your search and selection process early.

You may also consider being part of the solution in regions where supply can't meet the growing demand. In communities across the country, like-minded parents are gathering to develop housing options themselves, ranging from renting an apartment together to purchasing a home for their adult children to forming a local community housing option. Innovative choices include creating homes or neighborhoods cohabitated by members of the disability and senior citizen communities along with neurotypical people, fostering an inclusive environment for everyone. Developing the plans, support, and membership for such endeavors can be complicated. Consider engaging with organizations such as the Autism Housing Network that are prepared to develop new options for all with disabilities.

Caregivers and Guardians

There is a distinct difference between caregivers and guardians that is highlighted by the different approaches represented in this chapter. Dictionary.com defines a guardian as *"a person who guards, protects, or preserves,"* often through a legal decree. A caregiver is defined as *"a person who cares for someone."*

As a parent, you may always be a guardian for your person with Down syndrome although you may opt to transfer guardianship to your self-advocate or a relative at some point. A guardian often oversees their loved one's medical, financial, and housing arrangements including negotiations, communications, and decision making. Guardians should be knowledgeable of these areas and/or engage with professionals to protect and preserve the rights of the self-advocate.

Typically, parents are also the primary caregivers for their children, caring for their personal needs, helping to grow their skills, and teaching them how to apply those talents in the world. These responsibilities include providing or arranging for continuing education, vocational opportunities, and social integration to support your loved one's growth and development.

If your adult with Down syndrome lives in your home, you are likely the guardian and caregiver. If they move into any community-based home, the caregiver role transfers either to the self-advocate in the case of consumer-directed housing or to the agency or staff of the residential living community in the case of provider-directed housing. Both roles are critical for your loved one's success. Be sure to consider your interest and ability in providing these roles based on your housing choices. Also be sure to consider who will fulfill these roles in the future.

My wife and I evaluated the options in this chapter, ultimately opting for an assisted-living community for Gwendolyn in 2021. Not only does this situation provide Gwendolyn with social interaction and growth opportunities in a nurturing yet independent environment, it allows Jennifer and me to enjoy our retirement ambitions. Because we live only eighteen minutes away, we remain an important part of Gwendolyn's life. We also want to make sure Gwendolyn's siblings, Maddie and Noah, will not have to bear the responsibilities of being caregivers for Gwendolyn as they establish their own families and careers. That said, as you can tell from Maddie's story below, she maintains a close relationship with Gwendolyn and continues to ponder the role she may wish to play in the future.

Family Feature
Maddie's Story

"This is Maddie, my big-little sister!" Gwendolyn exclaims with a blooming smile. "Big-little sister," a title I wear with pride. I am her big-little sister because I tower over her at 5'2" to her 4'8", but I am also thirteen months younger than her. She is very protective over me, and in different ways, I am protective of her.

From as early as I can remember, I had a built-in buddy—someone to share the swing with when we were toddlers, someone to potty train with as an itty bitty. Growing up, we pretended to be twins more often than not. As kids, we were gifted matching clothing and dolls, and our names even rhyme, Madolyn and Gwendolyn. As far as Gwen and I were concerned, we were twins—twins that were thirteen months apart. Our parents tell us how we met most of our early childhood milestones together—I walked and so did she, I played and so did she. I went to school, and she did too. I always recognized there was something "different" about her classroom, though I couldn't pinpoint it until I was around eight.

I have always been protective of my little-big sister. Helping her play with toys and holding her hand as we walked—a task she wasn't so fond of. Growing up, Gwen never liked to walk further than a few hundred feet. She would choose her spot and stop in her tracks, stomping her feet and pouting to tell us she was done. Nothing, aside from candy, would incentivize her to continue walking. We went through our family ritual of helping encourage her to walk, telling her what privileges she would lose out on if she continued in her stubborn fog. But I had a trick up my sleeve, a trick that worked when we were six and seven, and a trick that works to this day. I would walk up to my sister, hold her hand and say, "Good sister? Remember we are twins? And twins stay together." I would give her hand a squeeze, a soft smile, and soon her little feet would start to shuffle down the sidewalk, her footsteps falling into rhythm with mine. I've used that trick more times than I can count. It's our (almost) twin telepathy. It's little moments like those that I still remember, where Gwen has helped shape me into the adult I am today.

From an early age, I knew I needed to advocate for my sister, to other children, to adults, and to her teachers. It helped that I wasn't a particularly shy kid. I remember clearly one year we were trying out a new religious school program on Sunday mornings. At the time, the new synagogue didn't have a class dedicated to children with disabilities. Eight-year-old me was ecstatic to find out that Gwen and I were assigned the same classroom—an excitement that was followed quickly with the realization of the responsibility to protect my sister from our new classmates and new teacher who didn't quite understand how to reach my sister. The teacher handed out the first assignment, one that was on par with my learning needs but was completely inaccessible to my sister's. Gwen sat and fiddled with her colored pens as I completed the assignment, checking in on her periodically to see her progress. It occurred to me she hadn't written anything. She was only interested in counting the pens and grouping them by color. I instinctively flipped the paper over and wrote out the names of the colors she had collected, creating an exercise in color matching where she could match the ink color to the color name I wrote on the paper.

I was so determined to give Gwen an activity that made her feel included that I failed to realize the gaze of our teacher, standing over our table. She quickly grabbed the pens, took our papers, and explained her disappointment that we weren't focused on the task she provided. I got in trouble that day, and I don't recall having Gwen as a classmate again after that. At that age, I didn't understand that teachers could be wrong, and school systems could be faulty. All I knew was that my sister wasn't being included, and that the room wasn't willing to adapt.

Growing up, we were lucky to be exposed to services and programs that did strive to include everyone, regardless of ability and adaptation needs. We attended summer camps designed for kids with disabilities and their siblings, an oasis where I didn't feel like I had to translate or hover for Gwen to feel included and welcome. I frequently sat with my sister's life skills class in the lunchroom in middle school, an opportunity for me to meet my sister's friends and see her interact with her small social circle. In high school, I often brought my sister to my after-school choir rehearsals. My friends were always enthusiastic and excited to meet Gwen, but very hesitant to actually interact and talk *to* her and not *about* her—the hesitation, I realized, sparked from apprehension and carefulness, usually not malice.

My hyper-awareness of inclusion as a kid has definitely fostered my mindfulness as an adult. In my work as a theatrical stage manager, I've been told my patience and understanding with people is far stronger than normal, probably stemming from the early days of getting my sister to walk with our family throughout our travels in Europe. I've been told my read on a room is pretty accurate, probably stemming from the needs my sisters and her friends required in a sea of staring eyes. I began to understand what people were actually trying to communicate but were too scared or anxious to say out loud. I try to see the good in everyone and take the time to find the good in those who have been "othered," and I never underestimate the power of a soft smile and a little hand squeeze.

Future things are weird to talk about. I have always known there will come a time when my parents won't be around to oversee Gwen's care, but who wants to think about their parents dying? The subject is taboo, and so is the subject of caregiving for an aging sibling.

I have lots of hopes for Gwendolyn. I hope she finds friends, maybe love, a sense of belonging and purpose. I've had long chats with my dad about what my sister's future could look like. She is currently in her second year at a residential community that caters especially for semi-independent adults with disabilities. Gwen has always craved independence—her own apartment, her own schedule.

Looking towards the future, I am both excited and scared for what is to come. I have always known that one day, Gwen will be my responsibility, a fact that is daunting, but is softened by the work that my parents have done to create a community for my sister and a sense of stability that will guide her through the transitions that adulthood brings. As I begin to navigate my path in the adult world, I can't help but plan for where my sister would fit in.

My fiancée and I dream about having a guesthouse for Gwen to live in part time. Life takes weird, unexpected turns, and while Gwen is set up for success at her residential program, who knows what twists and turns could lead to her taking residence with us.

While I can sit and daydream about welcoming Gwen into our home, I know I would have a steep learning curve to navigate doctors' appointments, therapists, and psychiatrists while balancing her busy schedule of work and enrichment, her social life, daily hygiene, and healthy eating habits.

The list goes on and on. Lurking in the back of my mind is the fact that Gwen may likely develop dementia, which only adds to the spaghetti soup of things to keep inline for her to have a good quality of life. I am fortunate that my parents are so proactive in Gwen's journey. I only hope that in time, I will be able to provide the support system for my sister, whether from afar or within our shared home. Thanks, Dad, for writing this book, I know it will be an invaluable resource for me when the torch is passed.

Maddie, Gwendolyn's sister

Chapter 13
Amenities & Considerations

The previous chapter laid out a wide range of home living options. As you ponder which arrangements may be best for your self-advocate, this chapter offers important criteria to consider in your deliberations. If you are leaning toward independence within the family home, this list will help you consider your caregiver role and how to structure activities to stretch your self-advocate's level of independence. If you expect to search with your self-advocate for a home of their own, this list will provide the criteria by which to evaluate the many residential living options that may be available in your community or beyond.

Level of Independence

We spent this entire book discussing ways to expand your self-advocate's independence. Now it's time to evaluate their progress in determining what level of independence you are looking for in a new home. Does the self-advocate want to cook and clean on their own? Make all their meals? Take and reorder any medications on their own? Or perhaps they need someone to pop in once or twice a day to check-in and provide some reminders? Maybe they need access to 24/7 support to cook their meals, administer meds, and ensure they get up on time? What support will your self-advocate need to have a flourishing experience?

It is critical to gauge the right level of independence your loved one is ready for: too much and you may feel they are not safe or secure, too little independence and they may feel stifled, unable to grow through plateaus and reach their dreams. Envisioning exercises can help you and your loved one to picture what life might be like, the role they can comfortably play, and the degree of independence you both are confident is correct. This process will become quite handy in narrowing down your choices.

Separating home living and day programs can be difficult. These two provide the backbone for your self-advocate's activities, interfaces, and growth. While we covered day programs and other postsecondary education options in chapter 9, you may also include many of the considerations below in evaluating continuing education choices.

Keep in mind, this does not have to be the one and only time you make independent living decisions. Over the years ahead, your self-advocate will grow, perhaps becoming ready to spread their wings further, warranting another consideration of the options in chapter 12 and here in chapter 13.

Evaluation Process

The process of choosing programs is like shopping for a home or car or considering a major life choice. What are you looking for? Now is the time to consider what is most important so you can be prepared for a thorough and productive evaluation of options. Below we will first address core priorities. These are high priority items which you may deem requirements. Next, we will review life enhancements or options that vary among housing alternatives, the importance of which depends on your self-advocate's interests and abilities. The Housing Evaluation Template provided at http://

<u>www.beyonddownsyndrome.net/The-Essential-Guide</u> will help you organize and simplify this process.

Core Priorities

There are many items to consider during your process. However, these five rise to the top. Yes, families may have slightly different definitions or expectations of each, but these items must be addressed whether at the family home or out in the community.

1. **Safety and Security**: We already discussed the importance of developing awareness and skills in this area in chapter 6. Based on your loved one's ability to make good choices and guard against risks, you may choose different levels of security. Some homes may have little—just a house or apartment with a lock. You may be able to augment that with an alarm system that your self-advocate can learn how to manage. More structured communities may have fences, gates, check-in procedures, and even chipped arm bracelets for residents so staff know where they are at all times. Some communities opt to minimize these measures to blend into the surrounding community, providing a greater sense of independence for the residents. You must also recognize that verbal, physical, and sexual abuse is rampant"[77] within the disability community. Consider this in terms of who your loved one engages with, and if they might be alone with others. Look for precautions and safeguards to protect your loved one. You will need to decide what level of security is adequate to keep your loved one safe and you sleeping well at night.

2. **Communication**: In this case, we are focusing on communication with those responsible for your loved one

each day, whether that is a day program, work location, social gathering, or living community. Your loved one should be out and about most days in order to grow, build a variety of experiences, and be an inclusive part of their environment. Engagement in the world creates a certain level of risk and communication is critical in mitigating those fears. You may be nearby, but it will take time for both your loved one and yourself to get used to being separate. If your loved one is in a consumer-directed housing option, you depend mainly upon your loved one to share their needs and concerns. If your own self-advocate is not highly communicative or limited in what they want to disclose, shared homes or provider-directed housing may be most suitable as it offers augmented communication through others. What communication are you looking for? You should certainly want the staff to communicate in a respectful and inclusive way with your loved one—they are the center of your plan. We conducted our housing search in several phases, described later. Be sure your self-advocate joins you for one of the tours. Observe how the staff includes your loved one in the discussions as well as the comfort level of your loved one. Interface on the tour may be limited to a few community representatives, but it's often a good indicator of the culture of the community. As parents/guardians, you will also want timely and transparent communication from the community, both about the general activities or issues (e.g., pandemic infections, outings, security issues) and updates regarding your loved one (e.g., how they are doing, personal issues, when they are sick, what classes they are taking, upcoming changes). Communications should both highlight successes and progress and make note of any concerns and how they are addressing them. Ask about these lines of communications during your discussions with day programs and living arrangements. Gauge how quickly and openly they address your questions during your tour, as well as by phone and email before and after. If communication is poor before you sign up, it will likely be even worse once you have committed and they have your business. Conversely, timely and transparent communication that is pervasive in their culture will shine through in everything they do. They should demonstrate this throughout your tour, even before you have a chance to ask.

3. **Health and Medical:** Ensuring good health and preparing for emergencies is important, whether your loved one lives with the family or on their own. For consumer-directed options, this responsibility lies with your self-advocate and yourself as caregiver. Some day programs and housing have on-site registered nursing staff and others do not. Who administers medicines to program participants? Who attends to someone who feels ill or trips and falls? What is their policy for contacting parents in any of these cases? Is exercise encouraged or required as part of their everyday routine? Do they have fun activities that your loved one would enjoy (perhaps basketball, swimming, dancing, and treadmill)? Do they have air conditioning and/or heating to ensure everyone is comfortable? Who takes them to routine doctor visits or sick calls? Be sure you are clear on these scenarios and arrangements, whether you or others are the primary caregiver.

4. **Location**: This criterion should be interpreted a number of ways:

   a. What is the physical location of their work, day program, or social gathering? Are they convenient for you to shuttle to or are there other transportation accommodations? If you are considering community-based living, do you want it to be within fifteen minutes or one hour of your home? Perhaps you are okay remaining remote if the right place is in another city. However, maybe you would relocate to be near your loved one once you find the right place, in which case you need to consider a whole list of criteria for a new family home.

   b. Does your self-advocate prefer to be in the city or in a more rural setting? This preference may affect the degree of security you require of the new community. It may also have a bearing on the types of day program activities available.

   c. Does the living community also have a day program and/or work opportunities at the same location or would your loved one be commuting every day? Who would provide, coordinate, and pay for such transportation?

5. **Costs**: There are generally two models for paying for day programs and housing. One is public through two state-run Medicaid waiver programs—one for routine support (day programs, therapy, respite care, adaptive communication devices) and the other for more substantial, longer-term care including housing. As mentioned in the finance and legal chapter, all states offer such programs but nearly all are fraught with either long waiting lists ranging from a few years to decades or low funding that only pays for

a portion of expected costs. The other payment plan is private—you fund these costs out of your pocket and/or with the other benefits such as SSI, HIPP, SNAP, and self-advocate earnings, as described in chapter 8. Depending on your state, the services your self-advocate requires, and the options available, day programs can cost $500 per month and up and housing can cost $1,000 to $5,000 per month and more. These costs can be astronomical, especially when you consider they are lifetime costs. Again, we must place an emphasis on getting on Medicaid waiver lists immediately and also planning and saving just as you might for a child's college fund. Many day and housing programs accept Medicaid waiver benefits while others do not, requiring private pay. In all cases, ask about acceptable funding mechanisms, along with any foundation- or grant-based scholarships that might be available. Cost is an important area to understand but doesn't have to deter you from your Independence Plan. With a thorough understanding and preparation through savings and early waiver program signup, you will have options. Without advanced planning, you may have none.

These five criteria are essential in determining both family home vs. community-based living choices as well as day programs for your self-advocate. The housing options offer varying degrees of service, but most families have particular views and expectations regarding safety, communications, health, location, and costs.

Life Enhancements

Regardless of your loved one's residential choice, the remaining criteria can be considered life *enhancements*. They make your self-advocate's days more interesting and exciting, build their independence skill set, and enhance their people skills and social circles. These criteria are subjective based on the interests of your self-advocate. You may not be able to address all of them yourself or find a residential community that attends to all these needs, so you may have to evaluate this list based on the most important activities for your loved one.

1. **Day Programs**: As covered in the education chapter, your self-advocate should continue to learn and remain challenged. This can be through work alone but often happens in combination with a day program. Day programs range from what appears to be babysitting to a pseudo–sweat shop. I suggest you look for programs combining educational, vocational, and social development. The participants' experience may include hygiene or life skills, indoor/outdoor activities, hobby classes like cooking, jewelry making, or painting, and field trips to fun events like parks, concerts, sporting events, and restaurants, along with learning places like factories or shopping. Look for a broad array of activities, offering fun learning and growth. During your fact-finding visit, ask questions about staff-to-attendee ratio, weekly schedules, and typical days. Be sure to observe the participants during your tour. Do they appear lively? Do they engage positively with the staff and vice versa? Does the program include exercises and a well-balanced variety of classes each week? If your loved one will be living in a residential community, does it have its

own day program? Is it located on the residential campus or is transportation provided?

2. **Housekeeping**: Who cleans their bedroom, bathroom, and social areas? Who does their laundry? Who cleans their dishes? While it might sound nice to the self-advocate if the housing community or parent does all that, I'd rather my loved one have these responsibilities, with proper oversight, to help build their life skill set and independence. As you tour, make note of the cleanliness and order of the bedrooms, classrooms, and other public areas. Cleanliness often reflects the organization and priorities of the community itself and those who run it.

3. **Meals**: Depending on the duration of the day program, are meals provided or will your loved one bring their meals and snacks? Do day and residential programs provide meals with a healthy balance and the proper portion size, or is it a buffet without many healthy choices or quantity monitoring? Is there an open kitchen or canteen residents can visit during the day or night to grab a snack? Can they accommodate specialty diets like lactose intolerant, gluten-free, vegan, or low carb/calorie options? What variety do they offer throughout the day and week? I certainly don't want my loved one to starve or be bored with the same menu or variety of sandwiches every day. I want them to be encouraged to drink water throughout the day and have access to healthy fruits, but I don't want them to be snacking all day and night.

4. **Sociability**: If they stay home, be sure to create social opportunities via playdates, social groups, and activities with peers. Day programs and residential homes should provide a

wide variety of social opportunities beyond just sitting next to someone. This is their chance to expand communication skills and develop trusting relationships that boost their self-esteem and mental wellness. Understand if your loved one can choose roommates and if they accommodate couples, including married spouses.

5. **Community Integration:** Everyone may have different aspirations here. Some families strive for full integration within the community at large. They resist I/DD residential communities and seek those in broader society or at least mixed residences within a neighborhood. Others find a quality day program and residential living community best meet their self-advocate's needs while still offering community integration through work and field trips. Consider your self-advocate's preferences and inquire with the day programs and homes about the opportunities that match your goals.

6. **Continuing Education:** To avoid the regression syndrome and extended plateaus that we discussed early, as well as to create a sense of confidence and pride, the day program and new independent home should present opportunities to develop and grow. Do they offer a wide variety of programs, social activities, and work opportunities? Will your self-advocate have a chance to exert their independence in different ways—through chores and work that expand as they grow? Might they have the opportunity to move from a dorm-like setting with roommates to a more independent suite-like arrangement down the road? Even for the most prepared self-advocate (and family), moving can be overwhelming. Continuing education helps them to

move off future plateaus while remaining at the same day program or home. Rest assured, there will come a day when a monotonous routine becomes boring. Seek those day programs and homes that offer growth in the years ahead.

7. **Work**: Even if a job is only a couple of hours a week, the responsibility of work and the pride it instills is priceless. You may be able to, or even need to, find your own work options for your self-advocate, but ideally the day program or living community either offers work options on campus (in the office, kitchen, or outside), has associated working options (a campus coffee shop or a packaging and shipping company that employs residents), or will help find nearby off campus job opportunities for which they will provide training and transportation. Things fall through the cracks due to poor communication. If the community itself is providing residency, day programs, work, and meals, chances are communications is excellent and such risks are minimized.

Sustainability

Develop your initial Independence Plan early on—when your loved one is a toddler. Keep updating it as your person-centered planning evolves, skill sets develop, and you all gain a better understanding of interests, options, and funding. Your plan may be to find the right day program when high school eligibility concludes or a home with an appropriate level of independence in their twenties or thirties. Your search for these two programs may continue as their abilities and needs change.

Your funding picture may change when you, the parents, start receiving Social Security, if money is allocated to your loved one through a special needs trust, or when you get off the Medicaid waiver waitlist. Any of these events could facilitate a move to another program or home down the road. Alternatively, you may seek a long-term option for your loved one to avoid having to put your self-advocate (and yourself) through the search process again and again. Consider your view on this to determine your objectives. If you are signing a contract on what is likely a shorter-term option (five to ten years), understand how you can move out of the community if you choose to down the road. If this is intended to be a long-term (twenty years to balance of life) option, ask about assisted living, nursing care, and memory care options at the community.

As mentioned in our health chapter, the preponderance of our community will deal with Alzheimer's before they are fifty, yet the average life span for people with Down syndrome continues to grow into their sixties and beyond. Will you or the day program and residential community be able to address those needs if/when the time comes, or will a move be necessary down the road? If the latter, who will help evaluate and make decisions with your self-advocate about these options? This would typically be their guardian—likely yourself currently, but perhaps someone else in the years and decades ahead. Whoever may assume that role should clearly understand your wishes and those of your self-advocate, as well as the steps and funding situation well before taking on this responsibility. Do not assume you will always be around or capable of being the guardian in the future. We all want smooth transitions for our loved ones. That is one key reason why you are planning for independence and conducting a thorough search in advance of your target date. You and/or the future guardian should continue this approach so your loved one and others are not caught in an unforeseeable emergency situation dictated by changing medical or financial conditions.

There are so many considerations before you begin your search. Similar to when you are searching for your next car or house, consider each of the criteria described in this chapter—determining which are critical and which are enhancements or not important—*before* you begin your search. Doing this work will help you form questions and objectives for tours and community discussions, narrow the list of options to a reasonable short-list, and make the final decision apparent when stacked up against these criteria and your priorities.

Rebekah shares her heartwarming story of goal setting and support to help Dutch gain employment and a place of his own.

Family Feature
Dutch's Story

Dutch was born in 1996 when I was just nineteen and newly married. When he was two days old the doctor suspected he had Down syndrome.

My first thought was "oh well, he can grow up and be anything he wants to be." That was because when I was growing up, we watched a show called *Life Goes On* with Corky, a man with Down syndrome as the main character. My mom always told us that people with disabilities could do anything.

So right from day one Dutch was determined—he survived heart surgery with infections, many trips to doctors, pneumonia, and an endless ear infection. He NEVER gave up, never complained, and was always smiling.

I did my part as well. I never babied him. I worked hard with him when he was younger on his fine and gross motor skills. I treated him the same as my other three children. Dutch grew up with two twin brothers and a sister five to six years younger than him, so he learned a lot from them. Dutch participated in every sport possible. He has always been very stubborn and determined so if he wants to do something, he figures out how to do it.

Dutch has always been extremely social. When he was sixteen, he started high school in a fairly new town, but it did not take him long to fit in and make friends, including one very special girl, Cheyenne. He didn't tell me about her for a couple of years because I used to joke that he couldn't get married until he was thirty-one. He also learned that he could move out when he was eighteen and get a job, so for the next three years he was packing frequently and telling me he was going to move out.

After graduating at nineteen, Dutch was registered with a local job agency in town and we wrote out his goals. After six months, Dutch had no job, no job training, and no discussion about employment. I asked them why and their answer was simple: "We don't want to set him up for failure." WHAT?? So, people with disabilities shouldn't experience failure? I removed him from that agency and decided to do family-managed supports, where I hire staff and the government pays for the services. I hired his first staff in July and Dutch had landed two jobs by his twentieth birthday in August.

He was working at a Tim Hortons location in our city two days a week for three years before new management took over and made some cuts to staff. He also got a job working for the city at our sports arena scanning tickets for sporting events and concerts including our local hockey team games. He isn't afraid to be around people or to ask for help. At work he greets patrons and learns from his coworkers. He doesn't hesitate to ask the bus drivers if this is the right bus for his destination for his commute. This has helped build capability and confidence.

Now Dutch still had one goal left to achieve—moving out. I did consider staffed community living for Dutch but there are limited options in our area, and I felt like he could do more. I didn't want him at a place that decided what he could and couldn't do. I want him to live life as he wants and to make his own decisions. The opportunity came up for him to move in with a support worker when he was twenty-one. We both interviewed support staff options to ensure it was the right fit for Dutch. He thrived with staff and learned so much.

Although as a mom letting go was hard, I never held him back and wasn't going to keep him from his dream. Two years later an opportunity came up that allowed us to purchase a home for Dutch.

I know I am not going to live forever, and he may outlive me. So, I need to make sure that Dutch has a home that belongs to him. We looked at a few properties, but the moment he stepped foot in that home he wanted it.

We live in a city and there are some rough and unsafe areas. So, choosing a home that would be safer was top priority. This home is in a quiet area with neighbors that look out for each other. Dutch is happy with his support roommate. He still needs reminders to take his thyroid meds and to wear his CPAP, but he is doing so well. He can take the city bus and do some shopping on his own. Cheyenne, his girlfriend of ten years now, comes over often, sometimes for sleepovers. His next goal is to marry her when they are thirty-one.

Rebekah, Dutch's mom

Chapter 14
Search & Decision-Making Process

You are ready to search for that right place. Your journey thus far has surely been filled with anxiety and anticipation. No one's path is perfect, but it is the path you and your family are on. It is important to keep in mind that everyone is different—our skills, our abilities, our interests, and our dreams. That is what makes the search for the right place so personal. What is a great fit for one is not for another. While consumer-directed options are, by definition, uniquely created by the self-advocate and family, the steps below are essential in finding that right place within the provider-directed options in particular. We'll start by listing your core priorities and life enhancements, and then gather information to aid in your evaluation and decision-making process.

Listing Core Priorities and Life Enhancements

Return to chapter 13 on amenities and considerations. Review your list of core priorities. Now is the time to create a list that reflects the interests and abilities of your self-advocate and provides you with the comfort and confidence you demand. Once you start touring a wide variety of options, it is easy to get wrapped up in the emotions of a place. Your self-advocate falls in love with a place because they were doing art, or the tour guide is so personable with your family. While both these factors can be considered, don't let them distract you from the list of important considerations you have developed.

Validate the core priorities and life enhancements on your list. The core priorities are immovable. They might include out-of-pocket costs or the proximity to your home, safety and security measures, or the degree of independence provided. Ideally, having a smaller core priority list supports a longer list of options to consider, but this has to feel right to you. Develop the list. Talk about it. Sleep on it. Modify it as needed before your search begins, and then resist changing priorities without careful consideration.

Your life enhancements are the items you are flexible on. This is where your decision will come into focus. For those situations that meet your requirements, the ones that also meet most of your enhancements will stand out. For instance, your enhancements might include day program activities. Your self-advocate loves music, dancing, art, basketball, swimming, and horseback riding. Some places offer only one or two, others several of them. Some may offer art every day and others just once a week. Some don't offer basketball. Assess which are important and the quality of each.

Before you start your tours, sit down with your self-advocate and consider what would warrant a high score or a low score for each consideration on your list. Jot these criteria down. **It is important to dream big and aim for that ideal place, but everyone, most especially your self-advocate, must recognize you may have to compromise to find that right place.** Also, keep in mind that you may not find great places for your family very easily. That's okay. Ensure your search is as wide as possible. Be flexible but don't sacrifice important priorities.

Searching for Options

So how do you find a comprehensive list of housing options? There's good and bad news here. The full gambit of housing options for your loved one is woefully in short supply. It will take a long time to have an adequate supply of quality housing options for the I/DD community. Consider this step early so you can plan accordingly. Nevertheless, there is still a broad array of quality projects to consider today. Unfortunately, there is no single repository for all the options. Consider these resources:

- Check out the Autism Housing Network (https://www. autismhousingnetwork.org/) and their housing directory (https://www.autismhousingnetwork.org/housing/), which has a growing list of options along with a lot of metrics and descriptions for each. Though the name implies an autism focus, the website and the housing directory provide an excellent resource for families of all intellectual/developmental disabilities including Down syndrome.

- Discuss living situations at your local Down syndrome association. Ask other parents for options. Encourage the organization to bring in experts that focus on housing for the I/DD community. Your association could provide a great service by developing a comprehensive and updated list of local options.

- Attend a local I/DD transition fair or workshop. Many cities offer a one- or two-day workshop with speakers on a wide variety of topics including housing, along with vendors that can help build your list.

- National resources like the National Down Syndrome Society (www.ndss.org) and National Down Syndrome Congress (www.ndscenter.org), which have keen focus on independence and adulthood for advocates, are also great sources of information and options. Regional and national conventions will certainly broaden your perspective on independence planning and housing options.

- Simply searching the internet for disability, special needs, or I/DD housing in the cities or regions you are considering will return a near-exhaustive list. Also search on the keywords described in chapter 12 on housing options, such as group homes, living communities, assisted living, and shared housing will augment your search.

- Perhaps the options in your area are scarce or even nonexistent. Maybe you want to be part of the solution. Consider huddling with other families to design a new community option. This happens all the time, so don't be overwhelmed. There are examples to consider and consultants that can help guide you through the legal aspects, design, planning and marketing of this path.

Once you have built your list for the geographic area(s) of interest, organize your process before you begin to engage. You can use a notebook, but an Excel-type spreadsheet is ideal. Put all your core and life enhancement considerations down column A and your housing options across row 1. The spreadsheet may become large, but it will provide you with the structure to gather all the information necessary to make decisions. Once you have created the spreadsheet, you are ready to go to the next step. Find a free, downloadable template at http://www.beyonddownsyndrome. net/The-Essential-Guide.

Gathering Information

Now that you have your list of criteria and your housing options, it's time to do some preliminary investigations. Gather basic, publicly available information from housing websites to assess availability and quality and to narrow your search. Also, look for key information like how long they've been in existence, location, population, staff, and program descriptions.

Search for their mission and scan their website to get a feel for the organization and culture. Is the website well made? This may seem irrelevant, but a sloppy or abbreviated website can speak to their quality of communication and attention to detail. Look for images that provide some insight into the community, staff and residents' happiness and friendliness, and the variety of activities. You would think every place would ensure an uplifting image, at least on their website, but you may be surprised and disappointed by some.

After you scour their websites, check out other sources such as the Better Business Bureau, your local Down syndrome organization, and the Autism Housing Network described above. Search for the community's name and see if you find other articles, reviews, or comments about them from the press, residents and families, former employees, and independent organizations. As we know, no one gets 100 percent five-star reviews, but a negative trend should be worrying.

Finally, ask other parents if they have heard of each place. If they have recently gone through a search, who was on their short list and the ultimate choice? Why did they eliminate other communities from their search? Later you can ask each housing option for some references you can talk to about their experience.

This investigation may take about thirty minutes for each location and is well worth it. You may have three or thirty on your list of housing options depending on your geographic area. This step will help you narrow down that large list and it will also highlight items that stand out as strengths and others that are suspect. You will then want to test both during your tours with observations and questions. Inconsistencies warrant further investigation. For instance, if the website or another family talk about the great day program yet your tour reveals a warehouse-type layout with unattended residents coloring in silence, ask questions until your seeds of doubt are either validated or refuted to your satisfaction.

Touring

Once you have completed your cursory investigations, schedule your tour for those that remain. Jennifer and I chose to do the initial tour without Gwendolyn, so we didn't overwhelm her with options and emotions. We then brought her to our short list for a second visit. You may have an exclusive tour or a standard, group tour. Some will be led by a manager or director and others by front line staff. Make the most of either situation and be prepared to follow up later.

You probably aren't going to visit with your laptop in hand, working off your spreadsheet of considerations. **Your job on the tour, after all, is to keenly observe and ask pointed questions.** However, do come prepared. This is your best chance to gather more information to complete your checklist, so you understand how each residential community meets or falls short of your considerations. Bring a small notebook of questions. Delve into any areas of concern or inconsistency from your initial data gathering. Ideally, come with a partner so one of you can check the list and take notes while the other asks questions and observes. Write down your thoughts and observations. There will be too much going on to try to remember it all when you debrief later. Put an asterisk next to those items you might want to follow up on, either with the tour guide, management, or some other independent resource or reference.

The most important aspect of your tour is observing the residents and the staff. This is the kind of information you really can't get from a website. Do the residents appear happy and engaged? Are there many different activities going on at the same time? Do they run up and hug the tour guide or other staff or do they bark out issues, e.g., "I'm hot," "I'm bored," "When can we leave or do something different?"

Day programs and residential communities are a melting pot, typically of a wide variety of abilities and interests. This diversity brings fun and joy to campus, but can also spark frustration, especially since many participants are not used to such numbers and diversity. How are the participants getting along? If you see issues, are they being addressed by staff in a kind and respectful way?

When touring group homes, you may be escorted by the agency that runs that home or a series of homes. That is fine but you also want to see the in-home caregiver and residents in action. How do they interact? Do they appear close or distanced? How do they divvy up the chores? What is a typical day like? What do they do at night and on weekends? What do they do if someone doesn't want to attend a group home outing or feels sick? How is security maintained? Who selects the caregiver and each resident? What are the criteria?

By the end of the tour, grab any brochures you see, ask for business cards, request a day program and outing schedule, and understand who you can follow up with later.

After the visit, spend some time with whomever joined you on the tour to debrief. Fill out the spreadsheet and add rows for new information. What appears inconsistent or of concern? Do you know enough to remove some from your list? Which have enough redeeming features that you want to test a few nagging concerns?

After your tour and debrief, your adrenaline may be flowing. Your curiosity regarding these concerns may be heightened. Before you follow up with your contact, I suggest that you sleep on it. If you are seeing more programs and communities that week, you may wish to join those tours before following up, so you can compare and contrast. Your observations may become clearer, which will help highlight key differences. The emotions may become more balanced with the facts and data you have gathered. The list of questions you have may lengthen. Then you will be ready to efficiently broach outstanding issues with each program.

Follow Up

Follow up on any concerns first by email. Not only will this help you think through your questions and review wording, but you get the answers in writing to fold into your spreadsheet. Perhaps most revealing from this email is the response time from the organization. People are busy, but if you don't get a response within twenty-four hours indicating they will at least get back to you soon, it is neither a satisfying answer to your questions nor a good reflection of the quality of communication you may expect in the future. If you don't hear from them in a day or two, you may give them one more chance and send a follow-up note or call them. Perhaps their response is to schedule a phone call or meeting to address your concerns and that is a quite satisfactory reply. Maybe you need another tour or meeting on campus to address any remaining gaps in your spreadsheet or nagging questions or concerns. Ask your short list for a few references—other families who may have made their decision across a broad timeline, from recently to years ago. Do what you need to do to ensure you have the information to drive the best decision.

Making Decisions

Once you have all the information you need, it is time to decide. Your spreadsheet should be full of data and metrics, observations, and perceptive remarks. Find a quiet place to review your list. Start with your core priorities. Factors like location/proximity, security, and degree of independence are addressed in different ways by the housing options on your short list. If they are truly requirements, any program that doesn't check all these boxes to your satisfaction should be removed. If you start to waiver on that, it may be because your requirements may be more flexible than you thought or because the other characteristics of that particular community are favorable. This is why we set these criteria *before* the tours: to remove the emotion from the process. But emotions, "feel," and intuition are indeed important. Challenge your core priorities if you feel the inclination to do so. Either way, sleep on it before recategorizing any requirements as flexible options. After such a review and any adjustments, remove those that don't meet your requirements from your short list. This may leave you with several to consider, maybe just one, or perhaps none. If you land on the first or third outcome, you have more work to do.

Several Options Remain

If several options remain, it's time to review the life enhancement options. As a family, discuss them individually and gauge the excitement or concern of each. No one place will have the quantity and quality of all the amenities on your list. Each will vary. Gauge what is most important. Help your self-advocate envision living there. What would their typical day be like? What will they talk about with excitement when you call or visit? What might they bemoan or miss? What does your intuition say? This is a big move. Don't let the difficulty of the decision deter you from the move itself but do make sure that your ultimate choice feels right to everyone. Again, rest on it and assess where your heart and mind are when you wake refreshed or have a couple of days to ponder. Once you land on the right place, you may wish to take one more tour or see if your loved one could be a guest for a few days or a week or attend a summer program on campus to confirm your choice and provide you with more peace of mind.

No Viable Alternatives

If, on the other hand, your review of requirements leaves you with no viable alternatives, review your core priorities once more. Perhaps you would consider broadening your geographic scope?

We started looking in our hometown of Houston. We expected such a large city would yield several alternatives, yet we found none that fit. We decided to travel to Dallas to visit other options and found one that was a strong contender. This obviously opened the possibility of relocating with Gwendolyn. We've always been adamant we want to be within thirty minutes of Gwendolyn so routine visits are feasible. Given we are both retired, we discussed it at length and felt a move out of Houston was both practical and exciting. Since that door was opened, we considered other geographic possibilities. We have family in Kansas City and Orlando, but a cursory look at the options didn't appear to provide an immediate fit. We were also reluctant to leave the state of Texas and give up our spot on the Medicaid waiver list for residential benefits in the future. However, during our discussions with Rosa Rocha, founder and leader of Gwendolyn's Houston day program, we were reminded of an option in Austin that she spoke highly of in the past. Once we toured Marbridge, just outside Austin, we knew we had found the right place for Gwendolyn. We reconsidered what a move away from our hometown of thirty years would look like and were excited about the prospects in Austin. Our process stalled due to the pandemic but resumed a year later with another tour, followed by an application and interview process, and placement on a waiting list.

Your own search may be similar or quite different. Test your assumptions and requirements; envision what changes to your list might yield. If your evaluation continues to yield no viable options, consider whether your requirements may change in the near future. Perhaps retirement will provide geographic flexibility? Maybe a prospect will be upgrading their facility or security measures? Some of your criteria may change or your sense of acceptability may evolve. Maybe new management will upgrade the culture of some establishments down the road. Perhaps your financial situation will change due to your RSDI or Medicaid waiver program accessibility. As you review your own process, I would encourage you to challenge your requirements but never to accept shortcomings that you and your loved one will regret.

If you opt to park your decision and wait, I urge you not to abandon the goal and process. Remember the objective is to find a great new home for your loved one that will help them grow and succeed, to enjoy personal development, confidence, and social connections. The other purpose of finding a sustainable option that enables a smooth transition instead of a burdensome, unplanned urgent search and move still remains. Depending on your own family circumstances, you may have time to reevaluate your options or await changing conditions, but this search for a new independent home for your self-advocate is too important to give up. There are new communities of many different styles being developed every year. You will find the right place that will leave you and your loved one excited, confident, and fulfilled.

Transition

You've made the decision. Congratulations! This is one of the toughest yet most poignant decisions of your life and that of your loved one. Don't let doubt or guilt creep in. Remember why you all started the independence journey in the first place. It's a great time to remind yourself of the person-centered planning principles. Your loved one is the focus and greatest beneficiary of your courage and hard work. Now it's important to make this transition as smooth as possible.

Engage with their new community about how they typically handle transitions. Depending on the style of option, maybe your loved one could go half days, full days, and then an overnight before fully moving in. Maybe a summer camp is the beginning of the full move to follow. For Gwendolyn, Marbridge had no partial-day options, and their summer camp was on pause due to the COVID-19 pandemic. In fact, we only had limited time to help her settle into her room while her roommate was away, given their pandemic protocols. The biggest challenge was the six-week no visitation policy. This has always been in place to shift a new resident's personal support team from family to community staff and co-residents. We were still able to call or FaceTime every night, so that made this period a lot easier. The fact she often called us about her meds or some other question or need confirmed the benefit of a stringent transition period. Nevertheless, the transition period can be an emotional adjustment for both the self-advocate and the family as a whole. However, over time we were confident Gwendolyn would enjoy her new surroundings and continue her own independence journey.

Family Feature
Gwendolyn's Story

As *The Essential Guide* prepared for publishing and Gwendolyn approached her fifteen-month anniversary at Marbridge, she and I sat down to talk independence.

Q: What does independence mean to you?

A: Taking care of myself and living on my own. Oh, and also eating healthier and exercising every day.

Q: Have you always wanted to live and work independently?

A: Yeah, since I was a tiny person.

Q: Who's the most important person in your Independence Plan?

A: Me, because I am special!

Q: Is everyone so independent?

A: Some people don't want to live on their own yet. That's okay. Some need some help. I need help with the laundry. I can't reach the bottom of the washer because I am short!

Q: What have you learned in the last five years of your independence journey?

A: I've learned to do things by myself, take care of myself, get along with others, and speak up for myself.

Q: Do your resident trainers help you out?

A: Yeah, they help me with laundry. They give me my pills and take me on town trips. And they help me if I'm not feeling well. They are nice!

Q: What are you learning at Marbridge?

A: To live with others and be a good friend. I don't like bullies. So, I kick rocks sometimes and stay with my friends. I have lots of friends here.

Q: What are your five favorite classes at Marbridge?

A: Pilates, basketball, personal hygiene, art, and writing.

Q: What are some new things you've done since moving?

A: Laundry, showering every morning without reminders, cleaning my room (sometimes), and biking around campus a lot. I'm making friends, hanging out, talking to each other, and going outside.

Q: Do you like working?

A: Yes. I need a job. [Marbridge waits a year or so after arriving to consider adding employment.] Firehouse Subs was my favorite job. I like to clean tables, wrap up brownies and cookies (I can't eat them), mopping, taking out trash, and making boxes. I like working with people and my boss, Heather. And I need money. [Shortly after our talk, she was awarded a job in the Marbridge cafeteria.]

Q: What kind of art do you do?

A: Drawing, painting, and making friendship bracelets. I sell them. I'm trying to have more money to spend on things I really need, like yarn, tape, and coloring books.

Q: You are quite the singer. How did you learn how to sing?

A: I am a singer. I learned from my brother. We are good singers. I sing really high. I am the rock star in the family. I sang at the [Friends of Down Syndrome's annual] Cinderella Ball, on a cruise, and at Marbridge karaoke Saturdays. My favorite singers are Lizzo, Alicia Keys, Dolly Parton, and rap.

Q: You are quite brave. What are you afraid of?

A: Three things. Heights, bugs, and hills. [She can't explain the last, but I think she just doesn't like walking up hills!]

Q: Are you happy?

A: Oh, yes! I am proud of myself.

Q: Do you miss living at home with Mom and Dad?

A: No.

Q: Do you miss anything?

A: Mom [she smirks and chuckles to herself and continues], and my sister [Maddie] and brother [Noah]…and their girlfriend and boyfriend.

Q: That's sweet. What about me?

A: A little [with a wide smile and sparkling eyes].

I love you too, Gwendolyn.

We are so proud of you. You are doing awesome!

CONCLUSION
Your Journey Ahead

This Project and guidebook have certainly transformed over the years, as have I. When we started, I was biased to the experiences of Gwendolyn and our family. I assumed our challenges mirrored the Down syndrome community. I expected this Guide would address the eighteen-plus transition to adulthood and the path we chose.

However, it has become so much more. Through the interaction with other families and experts, I've recognized everyone's path is different. One person's aspirations may be irrelevant to others. So, *The Essential Guide* has become just that, a guidebook for you to understand your options and choose your own path.

It has also become clear that the journey toward independence starts well before eighteen and, in fact, never ends. There is so much we can do for our loved one and ourselves as parents and caregivers to become aware of the possibilities and challenges and prepare as best we can for the glorious ride ahead.

I encourage you to celebrate your journey. Just reading this *Guide* underscores your commitment to independence and likely changes your family's path. I expect the depth of information can feel overwhelming at first. Use the resources gathered in this guidebook to smooth out the process. Prioritize your steps based upon the life stage of your self-advocate, their current skill set and abilities, and any upcoming life events. For example, if they are toddlers, focus on fostering independence in section II. If they are teenagers, familiarize yourselves with the foundations for the future in section III, especially as they approach age eighteen. If your self-advocate is around twenty, the opportunities to stretch into the community, as described in section IV, will beckon new possibilities and planning. And as your loved one becomes an adult with bigger needs and dreams, consider what independent living means to you.

The Essential Guide for Families with Down Syndrome may be pulled off your shelf as each life stage approaches. In the meantime, I hope that reading each section has calmed your fears, put your future in perspective, provided guardrails for the next phases, and instilled in your team the confidence that all the opportunities that await your loved one are indeed possible.

Epilogue

Gwendolyn has attended several one- and two-week summer camps over the years. But I will honestly tell you our eyes welled up while saying goodbye and as we sat in our car in the Marbridge parking lot afterward wondering what we had just done. However, that feeling quickly gave way to the surety that we did our due diligence in our evaluation and selection process and that this was indeed a great place for Gwendolyn. Later that day, our discomfort transformed to pride and a bit of excitement about our empty-nester status and the prospect of exploring our new hometown together.

During the six-week transition period, Gwendolyn did FaceTime us most nights, generally excited as she began to meet her new friends and enjoy the summer camp-like schedule of art, basketball, cooking, and jewelry classes. After six weeks, we enjoyed a great reunion, taking Gwendolyn out for her favorite dinner and some shopping while we caught up on all the news. We all celebrated the ultimate achievement of her Independence Plan!

In the months that followed, Gwendolyn has gotten into a rhythm on campus. We see her about every two weeks, usually alternating a dinner and shopping or movie outing with a weekend home visit. It's great to spend quality time with her and it's also nice to see her packed up on Sunday mornings, excited to return to her home.

The most challenging aspects of her move have been two-fold: medical and social. When Gwendolyn lived at home, Jennifer or I attended all of her doctor's visits to support and elaborate on the communication with the doctors and nurses. Now, there is a nurse on staff at Marbridge who attends to the occasional cough or ailment as well as periodic checkups. The nurse also coordinates routine primary care doctor visits, dental cleanings, and any needed specialty doctor appointments. We try to attend anything out of the ordinary, but we still want to be in the loop on the most routine of appointments. Despite the best efforts of the community nurse, this is a challenging transition for Jennifer and me. We are fortunate to be nearby, so we can join any appointments we feel necessary.

Socially, Gwendolyn struggles at times. She spent eight years at Houston's Friends of Down Syndrome where she was one of the original students in one of the more advanced classes. As a result, she had a lot of friends and carried a bit of swag within the school. When she first moved to Marbridge, she resided in a dorm with one roommate and dozens of others in the building. Gwendolyn's only other roommate had been her sister when they bunked together at around five years of age. Furthermore, she is the newbie on campus, so she has to find her way into conversations and friendship circles. She tended to be more communicative than most in the dorm, which was empowering but frustrating at times. Several months later, she relocated to a more independent-minded lodge with suitemates that were close-knit and often with more advanced abilities than she. This flipped the tables and has required some additional adaptation. She is making friends and enjoying her many classes, but at times she is sad or frustrated by social friction. Gwendolyn is an empath, so she picks up on the emotions of those around her. She can be sad when her friends are sad or when she interprets a comment or nudge as an affront or bullying rather than the spontaneous comment or accidental bump it was in reality. We remind her how far she's come and all the great things she loves about her new home.

Nevertheless, sometimes Gwendolyn wants to return to the simpler life of the dorm or even to Houston. We remind her that her move was not the end of her Independence Plan, just another big step on her life journey. To move environments is not to address the issue and grow, but to run and hide. History has taught us issues won't disappear and Gwendolyn won't learn to adapt to circumstances without addressing them. We are fortunate that she has a great support team within the community staff, an on-campus therapist familiar with these issues, and a loving family nearby. One of the key reasons we chose Marbridge was because of the compassion and communication we sensed during our tours and discussion. These are never more evident than now as we work together to help Gwendolyn continue to grow. We weren't sure what issues Gwendolyn, as a young lady, would encounter, but the support she is receiving is exactly why we all chose Marbridge in the first place.

Over a year after her move, Gwendolyn has adapted quite well. She had twenty friends at her campus birthday party, she is learning to "kick rocks" in response to the occasional rub and is happily busy with classes and social activities. We are all pleased with her adaptability and development this past year. She has great pride and satisfaction in her progress, and we are confident she will continue to learn and grow independently.

Steve, Gwendolyn's dad

Acknowledgments

The Essential Guide for Families with Down Syndrome has evolved in so many ways since its inception. It has been broadened by the shared experiences of so many families, strengthened by the contributions of experts, and sharpened by the talents of amazing editors and designers. Along the way, my own knowledge and passion for such a personal subject has illuminated in ways I could not have imagined.

I thank each of you not only for your magnificent offerings to the Guide, but also for the profound work you do with your self-advocate and family, with the Down syndrome and I/DD community, and with writers and authors seeking to get their work out there and help change the world.

Family Features: your stories stir, your courage inspires, your determination motivates. Thank you so much.

- Jonathan, father of Fionn
- Sheila, mother of Dale
- Maddie, sister of Gwendolyn Friedman
- Joyce, mother of Amanda
- Carolyn, mother of Daniel
- Rebekah, mother of Dutch
- Rosaura, mother of Ethan
- Larina, mother of Camille

- Stacy Lynn, mother of Slayton
- Heather, stepmother of Ayla
- Thora, mother of Chaya
- Stephanie, mother of Noah

Expert Advice: your knowledge and expertise has especially strengthened the safety and security, communications, education, health, and financial/legal chapters to provide the confidence for readers to tackle these critical areas.

- Sari Bar, D.O., Down Syndrome Clinic at Children's Health Dallas Campus, www.childrens.com/specialities-services/conditions/down-syndrome
- Calista Boyd, Friends of Down Syndrome, www.friendsofdownsyndrome.org
- Barbara Bush, Solutions for Special Needs Families, www.solutionssnf.com
- Betsy Furler, For All Abilities, www.forallabilities.com
- Tara Goodwin, D.O., QuestCare Medical Clinic, www.questcaremedicalclinic.com
- TJ Koehle, For Families of Special Needs, www.forfamiliesofspecialneeds.com
- Becca McPherson, Marbridge Foundation, www.marbridge.org
- Joseph Ryan, Ph.D., ClemsonLIFE, www.clemson.edu/education/programs/programs/culife

Beta Contributors: An amazing group of people dedicated hours to review and share their unique perspectives to the earliest manuscript draft to help reach out to the broad spectrum of the

Down syndrome community. Your impact is felt throughout the book.

- Joyce Cordell Gilmer, Ruth Hewitt, Carolyn Modawell, Heather Sellers, Arthur Volkmann, and Rebecca Weiner

Editors: Special appreciation to Anne Janzer who once again helped turned my thoughts and scribbles into prose with a purpose. I also want to acknowledge the contributions of my copy editor, Karen Jacot, who sharpened the flow and professionalism of my writing.

- Anne Janzer: www.annejanzer.com
- Karen Jacot: www.karenjacot.com

Graphic Designers: Alexander von Ness and Slim Rijeka of Ness Graphica, my cover designer and interior designer, once again converted my vision into the style that matches my words and purpose. My lovely wife, Jennifer, contributed her artistic talents to the silhouettes on the front cover.

- Ness Graphica: www.NessGraphica.com
- Jennifer Friedman: www.JennuineExpressions.com

Resources

These resources are provided to supplement your reading of The Essential Guide for Families with Down Syndrome and provide you with additional information for your family's journey.

Ch	Topic	Resource Company (Contact)	Website
3	Self-advocate business	Art with Heart (Amanda)	https://www.facebook.com/search/top?q=%40amandasartwithheartshop
4	Social relationships	Mad Hatter Wellness (Katie Thune)	www.madhatterwellness.com
4	Social activities	GiGi's Playhouse	https://gigisplayhouse.org/
4	National Down syndrome resource	National Down Syndrome Society	www.ndss.org
4	National Down syndrome resource	National Down Syndrome Congress	www.ndscenter.org
4	National I/DD resource	The Arc	http://www.thearc.org/
4	National I/DD resource	Easterseals	www.easterseals.com
4	Find a local Down syndrome association	National Down Syndrome Society directory	https://ndss.org/resources/local-support
4	Friendship/ mentoring	Best Buddies Program	https://www.bestbuddies.org/

Ch	Topic	Resource Company (Contact)	Website
4	Introversion resource	Beyond Introversion (Steve Friedman)	www.BeyondIntroversion.com
5	Mental health/ counseling services and resources	Rose Reif	www.rosereif.com
5	Communications & workplace disabilities issues	For All Abilities (Betsy Furler)	https://forallabilities.com/
6	Independent living community	Marbridge Foundation (Becca McPherson)	www.Marbridge.org
7	Down Syndrome Clinic Dallas	Adult Down Syndrome Clinic Questcare (Tara Goodwin, D.O.)	https://questcaremedical-clinic.com
7	Medical care guidelines for adults with Down syndrome	Global Down Syndrome Foundation's Medical Care Guidelines for Adults with Down Syndrome	www.globaldownsyndrome.org/medical-care-guidelines-for-adults/
7	Down syndrome research	LuMind IDSC Foundation	https://lumindidsc.org
7	Depression	Depression & Down Syndrome	https://www.communityinclusion.org/static/depression_DS_F2-28e8b15ba4573f5e0d95633db38bb06f.pdf
7	Mental health resource	The Diagnostic and Statistical Manual of Mental Disorders	https://www.amazon.com/Diagnostic-Manual-Intellectual-Disability-Diagnosis/dp/1572561319
7	Mental health resource	The Diagnostic Manual—Intellectual Disabilities 2	https://www.amazon.com/Diagnostic-Manual-Intellectual-Disability-Diagnosis/dp/1572561319

Ch	Topic	Resource Company (Contact)	Website
7	Alzheimer's disease	Alzheimer's Disease & Down Syndrome: A Practical Guidebook for Caregivers	https://ndss.org/resources/alzheimers
7	Dementia screening	National Task Group's Early Detection and Screening for Dementia (NTG-EDSD)	https://www.the-ntg.org/ntg-edsd
7	Down syndrome clinics	NDSC	https://www.ndsccenter.org/programs-resources/health-care/down-syndrome-clinics/
8	Financial advisor for special needs	Solutions for Special Needs Families (Barbara Bush)	www.solutionsforspecialneedsfamilies.com
8	Financial advisor for special needs	Life Planning for Families of Special Needs (TJ Kroehle)	www.forfamiliesofspecialneeds.com
8	Health insurance premium payment by state	HIPP	Google "HIPP" for your state
8	Social Security information	Social Security Administration	www.ssa.gov
8	Social Security information on retirement, survivorship, and disability insurance	SSA—RSDI	https://www.ssa.gov/privacy/pia/Retirement%20Survivors%20Disability%20Insurance%20Accounting%20System.updtd%20Sept%2028.htm
8	Social Security information on disability insurance	SSA-SSDI	https://www.ssa.gov/benefits/disability/

Ch	Topic	Resource Company (Contact)	Website
8	Medicaid social services/waiver program information	SSI/Medicaid by State	http://medicaidwaiver.org/state/vermont.html
8	ABLE account description and details	ABLE account	www.ablenow.com
8	ABLE to Work Act	Affecting annual contributions	https://www.ablerc.org/wp-content/uploads/2021/01/ABLE-ToWorkActFactsheet.pdf
8	SNAP directory	USDA Food & Nutrition Services	https://www.fns.usda.gov/snap/state-directory
9	Model day program	Friends of Down Syndrome (Karen Evans)	www.friendsofdownsyndrome.org
9	Model inclusive college program	ClemsonLIFE (Dr. Joe Ryan)	https://www.clemson.edu/education/programs/programs/culife/
9	Inclusive college program directory	Ivywise.com	https://www.ivywise.com/ivywise-knowledgebase/resources/article/colleges-with-programs-for-students-with-special-needs/
10	Vocational rehabilitation information	US Department of Education Vocational Rehabilitation	https://rsa.ed.gov/about/programs/vocational-rehabilitation-state-grants
10	Disability employment policy	US Department of Labor Office of Disability Employment Policy (ODEP)	https://www.dol.gov/agencies/odep
10	Job assistance	State's Workforce Commissions Directory	https://www.dol.gov/agencies/eta/wotc/contact/state-workforce-agencies
10	Self-advocate business	Fionnathan Productions	www.fionnathan.com

Ch	Topic	Resource Company (Contact)	Website
10	Self-advocate businesses	NDSC advocate businesses	https://www.ndsccenter.org/support-get-involved/shop-ndsc/self-advocate-marketplace/
10	Self-advocate businesses	NDSS advocate businesses	https://ndss.org/donate/shop-ndss
11	Navigating a Dual Diagnosis Down Syndrome and Autism Spectrum Disorder	Global Down Syndrome	https://www.globaldownsyndrome.org/navigating-dual-diagnosis-syndrome-autism/
11	Medical questions and community	Down Syndrome Diagnosis Network	https://www.dsdiagnosisnetwork.org/
12	Housing & community options	A Place in the World	https://www.autismhousingnetwork.org/apitw-report/
12	Housing consultancy	Autism Housing Network (Desiree Kameka Galloway)	www.autismhousingnetwork.org
14	Housing directory & guide	Autism Housing Network (Desiree Kameka Galloway)	https://www.autismhousingnetwork.org/apitw-report/

References

(Endnotes)

1   Alan H. Bittles, Carol Bower, Rafat Hussain, and Emma J. Glasson, "The Four Ages of Down Syndrome," *European Journal of Public Health,* vol 17, issue 3, April 2007, p 221-225, https://doi.org/10.1093/eurpub/ckl103.

2   "Facts and FAQ About Down Syndrome," Global Down Syndrome Foundation, 2018, https://www.globaldownsyndrome.org/about-down-syndrome/facts-about-down-syndrome/?gclid=CjwKCAiA9qKbBhAzEiwAS4yeDc0rRqhHubZdxyuGdO-KEiVxIY2tDVYGwz1fUi_mi3i2Z8S3TPYeCxoCtQcQAvD_BwE#facts.

3   Alan H. Bittles, Carol Bower, Rafat Hussain, and Emma J. Glasson, "The Four Ages of Down Syndrome," *European Journal of Public Health,* vol 17, issue 3, April 2007, p 221-225, https://doi.org/10.1093/eurpub/ckl103.

4   Steve Friedman, *UPL Family Survey* (Austin, TX: Peavine Press, 2022).

5   Denise D. Resnik and Desiree Kameka Galloway, eds., *A Place in the World: Fueling Housing and Community Options for Adults with Autism and Other Neurodiversities* (Phoenix, AZ: First Place AZ; Madison House Autism Foundation; the Arizona Board of Regents for and on behalf of Arizona State

University and its Morrison Institute for Public Policy at the Watts College of Public Service and Community Solutions, 2020), p 17.

6   Ariana Eunjung Cha, "Babies with Down Syndrome Are Taking Center Stage in the US Abortion Fight," *Washington Post,* March 5, 2018, https://www.washingtonpost.com/news/to-your-health/wp/2018/03/05/down-syndrome-babies-are-taking-center-stage-in-the-u-s-abortion-fight/.

7   Pamela Li, MS, MBA, "Formative Years – Why Are They Important in Child Development," Parenting for Brain, June 28, 2022, https://www.parentingforbrain.com/formative-years/.

8   Scott Mautz, "Psychology Says This Is the Top Contributor to Happiness (It's Not What You Think)," *Inc.,* February 2, 2017, https://www.inc.com/scott-mautz/psychology-says-this-is-the-top-contributor-to-happiness-its-not-what-you-think.html.

9   Steve Friedman, *UPL Family Survey* (Austin, TX: Peavine Press, 2022).

10 Eli A. Wolff and Dr. Mary Hums, "'Nothing About Us Without Us'—Mantra for a Movement," *Huffpost,* September 6, 2017, https://www.huffpost.com/entry/nothing-about-us-without-us-mantra-for-a-movement_b_59aea450e4b0c50640cd61cf.

11 Julie A. Moran, DO, *The Alzheimer's Disease & Down Syndrome Guidebook: A Practical Guidebook for Caregivers* (Washington, DC: National Down Syndrome Society, 2018), p 2.

12 PsychologyDictionary.org, April 7, 2013, "plateau."

13 Katie Thune, speaking at NDSS Adult Summit, "Supporting Healthy Relationships for 20 to 30 Year Olds with IDD," Dallas, TX, August 27, 2022.

14 Ibid.

15 Steve Friedman, "Caregivers of Adults with Down Syndrome Need This Info," NDSS' Virtual Adult Summit (2nd Half), Peavine Press, Austin, TX, June 2, 2020, https://www.beyonddownsyndrome.net/post/caregivers-of-adults-with-down-syndrome-need-this-info-ndss-virtual-adult-summit-2nd-half.

16 Steve Friedman, BeyondIntroversion.com (Austin, TX: Peavine Press, 2022).

17 Peter Wohlleben, *The Hidden Life of Trees: What They Feel, How They Communicate: Discoveries from a Secret World* (London, UK: William Collins, 2017), pp 6-13.

18 Steve Friedman, *UPL Family Survey* (Austin, TX: Peavine Press, 2022).

19 Carrie Clark, "Podcast: Communication-Based Behavior Problems," August 2013, https://www.speechandlanguagekids.com/slk12-communication-based-behavior-problems/.

20 Kitty-Rose Foley BSc, Jenny Bourke MPH, Stewart L. Einfeld MD, Bruce J. Tonge MD, Peter Jocoby MSc, and Helen Leonard MPH, "Patterns of Depressive Symptoms and Social Relating Behaviors Differ Over Time From Other Behavioral Domains for Young People with Down Syndrome," *Medicine,* vol. 94, issue 19, May 2015, https://journals.lww.com/md-journal/fulltext/2015/05030/patterns_of_depressive_symptoms_and_social.1.aspx.

21 Rose Reif, speaking at NDSS Adult Summit, "Helping Your Adult Child Understand Death and Cope with Grief—Workshop for Parents of Adult Children," Dallas, TX, August 27, 2022.

22 Ibid.

23 Betsy Furler, email message to author, September 7, 2022.

24 Ibid.

25 Ibid.

26 Ibid.

27 Alyssa Siegel, MD, "Keeping Your Special Needs Child Safe," Children's Hospital of Philadelphia (blog), August 30, 2018, https://www.chop.edu/news/keeping-your-special-needs-child-safe.

28 Desiree Kameka Galloway, "Once Size Does Not Fit All Video—Part II: Facing the Challenges for a Better Future," Madison House Autism Foundation, https://www.autismhousingnetwork.org/education/virtual-tour-housing-options/.

29 Kay Fendel, interview with the author, November 3, 2019.

30 Disability Justice, "Abuse and Exploitation of People with Developmental Disabilities," 2022, https://disabilityjustice.org/justice-denied/abuse-and-exploitation/.

31 The Administration for Community Living, "See Me for Me at Any Age: Celebrating Developmental Disabilities Awareness Month," 2018, https://acl.gov/news-and-events/acl-blog/see-me-me-any-age-celebrating-developmental-disabilities-awareness-month.

32 Tara Goodwin, M.O., personal interview and emails with the author, September 30, 2022.

33 Ibid.

34 L Chiovato, F Magri, and A Carle, "Hypothyroidism in Context: Where We've Been and Where We're Going," *Advances in Therapy,* 36 (Suppl 2), 2018, pp 47-58, https://doi.org/10.1007/s12325-019-01080-8.

35 AY Tsou, P Bulova, G Capone, et al, "Medical Care of Adults with Down Syndrome: A Clinical Guideline," *JAMA* 2020; 324 (150:1543-1556), 2020.

36 PE Peppard, T Young, JH Barnet, M Palta, EW Hagen, and KM Hla, "Increased Prevalence of Sleep-Disordered Breathing in Adults," *Am J Epidemiol,* 2013, pp 1006-1014.

37 MS Trois, GT Capone, JA Lutz, et al., "Obstructive Sleep Apnea in Adults with Down Syndrome," *Journal of Clinical Sleep Medicine,* 2009, pp 317-323.

38 Tara Goodwin, M.O., interview and emails with the author, September 30, 2022.

39 Steven M. Schwarz, MD, "Obesity in Children," *Medscape,* December 1, 2020, https://emedicine.medscape.com/article/985333-overview#:~:text=Obesity%20is%20the%20most%20prevalent%20nutritional%20disorder%20among,of%20obesity%20is%20highest%20among%20specific%20ethnic%20groups.

40 Rosette Gatt, "Obesity—How and why does it affect persons with Down syndrome?" Inspire: The Foundation for Inclusion, April 28, 2014, https://inspire.org.mt/down-syndrome-obesity/.

41 "Medical Care Guidelines for Adults with Down Syndrome," Global Down Syndrome Foundation, 2022, p 21, https://www. globaldownsyndrome.org/medical-care-guidelines-for-adults/.

42 Global Down Syndrome Foundation, "What You Should Know About Celiac Disease & Down Syndrome," *Down Syndrome World,* issue 3, September 28, 2021, https://www. globaldownsyndrome.org/what-you-should-know-about-celiac-disease-down-syndrome/#:~:text=About%201%25%20 to%203%25%20of,major%20long%20term%20health%20 impacts.

43 Kitty-Rose Foley BSc, Jenny Bourke MPH, Stewart L. Einfeld MD, Bruce J. Tonge MD, Peter Jacoby MSc, and Helen Leonard MPH, "Patterns of Depressive Symptoms and Social Relating Behaviors Differ Over Time From Other Behavioral Domains for Young People with Down Syndrome," *Medicine,* vol 94, issue 19, May 2015, https:// journals.lww.com/md-journal/fulltext/2015/05030/ patterns_of_depressive_symptoms_and_social.1.aspx.

44 "Medical Care Guidelines for Adults with Down Syndrome," Global Down Syndrome Foundation, 2022, p 15, https://www. globaldownsyndrome.org/medical-care-guidelines-for-adults/.

45 Rose Reif, speaking at NDSS Adult Summit, "Helping Your Adult Child Understand Death and Cope with Grief— Workshop for Parents of Adult Children," Dallas, TX, August 27, 2022.

46 Tara Goodwin, M.O., interview and emails with author, September 30, 2022.

47 *2022 Alzheimer's Disease Facts and Figures,* (Chicago: Alzheimer's Association, 2022), p 24.

48 "'Risks of Alzheimer's Disease in Adults with Down Syndrome' webinar and introduction to research study is March 29," Vanderbilt University, March 8, 2021, https://news.vanderbilt.edu/2021/03/08/risks-of-alzheimers-disease-in-adults-with-down-syndrome-webinar-and-introduction-to-research-study-is-march-29/.

49 Julie A. Moran, D.O., *Alzheimer's Disease & Down Syndrome: A Practical Guidebook for Caregivers,* (Washington, DC: NDSS, 2018), p 6.

50 Tara Goodwin, D.O., interview and emails with the author, September 30, 2022.

51 Ibid.

52 "Medical Care Guidelines for Adults with Down Syndrome," Global Down Syndrome Foundation, 2022, p 19, https://www.globaldownsyndrome.org/medical-care-guidelines-for-adults/.

53 NLF Diniz, E Parlato-Oliveira, PGA Pimenta, LA Arajujo, and ER Valadares, "Autism and Down Syndrome: Early Identification and Diagnosis," *Arq Neuropsiquiatr,* June 2022, https://pubmed.ncbi.nlm.nih.gov/35946706/.

54 Dr. Sari Bar, interviews and emails with the author, October 25, 2022.

55 Ibid.

56 Ibid.

57 Ibid.

58 Julie A. Moran, D.O., *The Alzheimer's Disease & Down Syndrome Guidebook: A Practical Guidebook for Caregivers* (Washington, DC: National Down Syndrome Society, 2018), pp 8-10.

59 Christine Mikstas, RD, LD, "Boost Your Metabolism," WedMD, November 4, 2021, www.webmd.com/diet/ss/slideshow-boost-your-metabolism#:~text=Power.

60 "Water: How much should you drink every day?," Mayo Clinic, October 12, 2022, www.mayoclinic.org/healthy-lifestyle/nutrition-and-healthy-eating/in-depth/water/art-20044256#

61 Denise D. Resnik and Desiree Kameka Galloway, eds., *A Place in the World: Fueling Housing and Community Options for Adults with Autism and Other Neurodiversities* (Phoenix, AZ: First Place AZ; Madison House Autism Foundation; the Arizona Board of Regents for and on behalf of Arizona State University and its Morrison Institute for Public Policy at the Watts College of Public Service and Community Solutions, 2020), p 19.

62 Barbara Bush, interviews and emails with the author, October 5, 6, and 21, 2022.

63 TJ Kroehle, interview with the author, October 5, 2022.

64 Denise D. Resnik and Desiree Kameka Galloway, eds., *A Place in the World: Fueling Housing and Community Options for Adults with Autism and Other Neurodiversities* (Phoenix, AZ: First Place AZ; Madison House Autism Foundation; the Arizona Board of Regents for and on behalf of Arizona State University and its Morrison Institute for Public Policy at the Watts College of Public Service and Community Solutions, 2020), p 18.

65 *Financial Wellness: A guide for individuals with disabilities, their families and caregivers* (Washington, DC: National Down Syndrome Society, 2021), p 31.

66 Ibid.

67 Brian Chicoine MD, "Regression and Loss of Skills in Adolescents and Adults with Down Syndrome Presentation," Advocate Medical Group: Adult Down Syndrome Center, February 17, 2020, https://adscresources.advocatehealth.com/ regression-and-loss-of-skills-in-adolescents-and-adults-with-down-syndrome-presentation-2172020/.

68 "Statistics to Share," Autism Housing Network, 2022, https://www.autismhousingnetwork.org/education/ statistics-to-share/.

69 Steve Friedman, *UPL Family Survey* (Austin, TX: Peavine Press, 2022).

70 Barbara Bush, interviews and emails with the author, October 5, 6, and 21, 2022.

71 Denise D. Resnik and Desiree Kameka Galloway, eds., *A Place in the World: Fueling Housing and Community Options for Adults with Autism and Other Neurodiversities* (Phoenix, AZ: First Place AZ; Madison House Autism Foundation; the Arizona Board of Regents for and on behalf of Arizona State University and its Morrison Institute for Public Policy at the Watts College of Public Service and Community Solutions, 2020), p 149.

72 Desiree Kameka Galloway, "Once Size Does Not Fit All Video— Part 3.1: Innovations Across the Country," Madison House Autism Foundation, https://www.autismhousingnetwork.org/ education/virtual-tour-housing-options/.

73 Steve Friedman, *UPL Family Survey* (Austin, TX: Peavine Press, 2022).

74 "Statistics to Share," Autism Housing Network, 2022, https://www.autismhousingnetwork.org/education/statistics-to-share/.

75 Denise D. Resnik and Desiree Kameka Galloway, eds., *A Place in the World: Fueling Housing and Community Options for Adults with Autism and Other Neurodiversities* (Phoenix, AZ: First Place AZ; Madison House Autism Foundation; the Arizona Board of Regents for and on behalf of Arizona State University and its Morrison Institute for Public Policy at the Watts College of Public Service and Community Solutions, 2020), p 21.

76 Desiree Kameka Galloway, interview with the author, July 12, 2022.

77 Desiree Kameka Galloway, "Once Size Does Not Fit All Video—Part II: Facing the Challenges for a Better Future," Madison House Autism Foundation, https://www.autismhousingnetwork.org/education/virtual-tour-housing-options/

Author Bio

The Essential Guide for Families with Down Syndrome is a personal passion project which has acted as a catalyst for engaging with many other families and experts with the aim of accelerating their journey toward independence.

I retired after thirty years in corporate America leading logistics and commercial teams in the energy industry. Suddenly, I had the opportunity to find a new calling. I reconnected with my teenage love of writing. Not only has it allowed me to align with my creative side, but writing has provided a vehicle for connecting with others and helping to make a difference.

My first two books—my memoir, *In Search of Courage*, and my leadership book, *The Corporate Introvert: How to Lead and Thrive with Confidence*—were projects of self-discovery and empowerment of others within the "hidden half."

My wife, Jennifer, and I are now enjoying the empty-nester lifestyle in Austin, Texas. Our oldest daughter, Gwendolyn, resides in an independent living community nearby, and we all relish visiting our other children, Maddie and Noah, who are scattered around the country.

I love hearing other families' stories and dreams. You can reach me on email and social media.

Email: BeyondDownSyndrome@gmail.com

Website: www.BeyondDownSyndrome.net

Facebook: www.facebook.com/BeyondDownSyndrome

Index

Made in the USA
Columbia, SC
15 February 2023